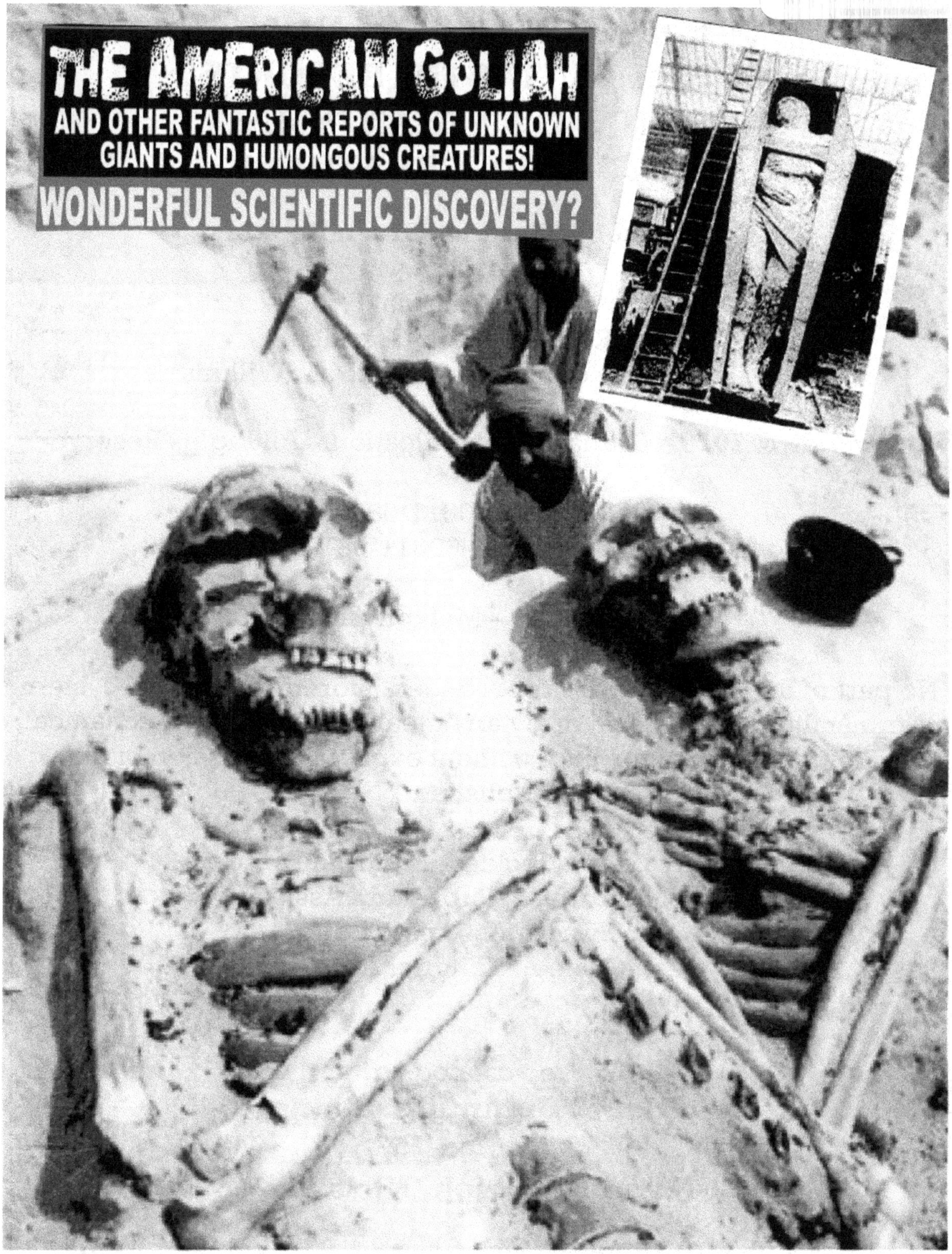

THE AMERICAN GOLIAH
AND OTHER FANTASTIC REPORTS OF UNKNOWN GIANTS AND HUMONGOUS CREATURES!
WONDERFUL SCIENTIFIC DISCOVERY?

GLOBAL COMMUNICATIONS

THE AMERICAN GOLIAH AND OTHER FANTASTIC REPORTS OF UNKNOWN GIANTS AND HUMONGOUS CREATURES

Compiled by Timothy Green Beckley

Additional Material by
Nick Redfern, Scott Corrales,
Andrew Dickson White, & Harold T. Wilkins

Copyright © 2010 – Global Communications, All Rights Reserved

ISBN-10: 1-60611-081-0
ISBN-13: 978-1-60611-081-2

Nonfiction – Metaphysics

No part of this book may be reproduced, stored in retrieval system or transmitted in any form or by any means, electronic, mechanical, photocopying, recording, without express permission of the publisher.

Timothy Green Beckley: Editorial Director
Carol Rodriguez: Publishers Assistant
Tim Swartz: Associate Editor
Sean Casteel: Editorial Assistant

For free catalog write:
Global Communications
P.O. Box 753
New Brunswick, NJ 08903

Free Subscription to Conspiracy Journal E-Mail Newsletter
www.conspiracyjournal.com

Contents

**Confronting The Not So Jolly -- Not At All Green – Giant
by Timothy Green Beckley** .... - 5 -

The Strange Tale of the Cardiff Giant by Nick Redfern .... - 9 -

The Persistence of Giants by Scott Corrales .... - 15 -
   An Uncomfortable Memory .... - 16 -
   The Codexes Speak .... - 18 -
   Giants of the South .... - 20 -
   Mad About Mu .... - 21 -
   Conclusion .... - 23 -

South American Giant Ufonauts by Scott Corrales .... - 25 -
   An Argentinean Giant .... - 25 -
   "Tallfellows" and Truck Drivers .... - 27 -
   Giants, Guards and Gunfire .... - 30 -
   Giants of Andalusia .... - 32 -
   Making Sense of it All .... - 33 -

The American Goliah by Anon. .... - 35 -
   The American Goliah A Wonderful Geological Discovery .... - 39 -
   Wonderful Scientific Discovery. A Giant Of Stone .... - 40 -
   Position of the Figure .... - 42 -
   What Is It? .... - 43 -
   Is The Body A Petrifaction? .... - 47 -
   What Is The Character Of The Surroundings Of The Image? .... - 50 -
   How To Find The Giant .... - 50 -
   Who Visits The Wonder? .... - 51 -
   How Long Will He Be Kept? Where He Was Found? .... - 51 -
   Who Owns The Image? .... - 52 -
   Letter Favoring Petrifaction .... - 59 -
   The Belief Of The Onondaga Indians The Body Of An Indian Prophet .. - 66 -
   The Stone Giant .... - 67 -
   Letter From A Petrifactionist .... - 68 -
   Opinion Of Professor Hall, State Geologist .... - 71 -
   More Than A Nine Days' Wonder .... - 74 -
   The Value Of The Giant Wonder .... - 75 -
   An Ancient Coin Found In The Earth Taken From The Giant's Bed .... - 75 -
   Probabilities That It Was Transported On The Water-Courses From The Sea-Board ...... - 76 -
   When Was The Statue Put Where It Was Found? .... - 77 -
   Of What School Of Art Is This Statue? .... - 78 -
   Cut Of The Giant .... - 81 -

A Mite In The Scale... - 82 -
Letter From Prof. Ward.. - 83 -
Letter From Gen. E. W. Leavenworth... - 88 -
Letter From Professor Hall, The State Geologist... - 91 -
To The Giant of Onondaga... - 92 -

The Cardiff Giant: A Chapter In The History Of Human Folly 1869-1870 by *Andrew Dickson White* .... - 95 -
Endnotes .... - 118 -

Strange Creatures and Monsters Galore by Harold T. Wilkins..................................- 121 -
Tall Tales Versus Scientific Skepticism .... - 122 -
Plateaux Of Western U.S. And "Lost World" Of Brazil .... - 123 -
J. Lerius Meets Monster Lizard On Island Near Rio.. - 124 -
Unicorns In The U.S.A.?... - 125 -
The Red Men Like Theirs Roasted .... - 126 -

Dinosaurs Haunt America ....- 129 -
Jefferson Reports On Fossil Of Pre-Historic Feline... - 129 -
"Megalonyx" Of Jefferson Encountered In The Flesh .... - 129 -
Old World Petroglyphs In Cave .... - 131 -
A Reptile "Mosqueto" Near Syracuse; A Horned Serpent Whose Stench Could Kill ..... - 133 -
Was Early Man Coeval With Dinosaurs? .... - 133 -
A Dinosaur Idol Found At Granby, California.. - 134 -
A Dinosaur Mummy Discovered In "Bad Lands" Of Wyoming .... - 134 -
Dinosaur Tracks Found Near Painted Desert .... - 135 -
Monster-Scared Indians Live In Lake Houses, Forts .... - 135 -

More American Dinosaurs..- 137 -
Pictographs Of Tyrannosaurus Unearthed In Arizona... - 137 -
Artifact Of Armoured Stegosaurus Type Found East Of Portland, Oregon .... - 137 -
Tall Tales From The Yukon Territory.. - 138 -
Speculation On The Myth Or Reality Of Modern Monsters .... - 142 -

King Kong Lives! ....- 143 -
Hairy King Kong Of Yucatan .... - 143 -
Hairy King Kong Disrobes And Shakes Up Mayan Women .... - 147 -
Teddy Roosevelt Makes Voyage Down "River Of Doubt".. - 147 -
Explorers Disappear During Search For Dead City .... - 148 -
Ape Man's Reign Of Terror On Rio Araguayan Border .... - 149 -
Sex Relations Between Giant Apes And Indian Women; Their Hybrid Progeny .... - 149 -

Anthropoids, Giants and Mammoths...- 151 -
Thaddeus O'shea's Non-Amorous Contact With Anthropoid .... - 151 -
Giant Men, Mammoths, Mastadons In Amero-Indian Myths .... - 153 -
Do Mastodons Still Live— And Shed Their Teeth In The Andes? .... - 156 -
Trader (Aloysius) Horn Sounds Off .... - 156 -
Mastodon Bones At Bottom Of Mine Shaft In Zululand .... - 157 -

Confronting The Not So Jolly -- Not At All Green – Giant
by Timothy Green Beckley

More than tired from an active day as a publisher, my mind was beginning to wander a bit. I couldn't help but think of a very strange e mail my friend and fellow writer Nick Redfern had sent me earlier. I was wandering across Manhattan's 23rd Street as the clock on the nearby Metropolitan Life Insurance building was about to strike midnight. Walking uptown on Madison Ave, I was rapidly approaching Madison Square Park when I noticed a stone-like figure standing on the sidewalk inside a fenced off area. I kind of chucked to myself as the statue (that's what I thought it was at first) sort of reminded me of an alien being someone had drawn to illustrate an article in my now defunct newsstand publication UFO UNIVERSE. Getting ever closer, the form looked perhaps even odder if that is at all possible. Certainly it wasn't an unknown invader from space that had stepped off a flying saucer in the middle of the night. Now within six feet of where it stood, the statue took on the appearance of a petrified or man made of stone.

To say I was mystified and awestruck simplifies the state of my being. Nick had just sent me an outline for an article on how a witness had observed a living, breathing, replica of the Cardiff Giant cross the road in several gigantic strides not far from where the original faked coleuses remains on display in an upstate NY museum.

Luckily, I had a tiny digital camera in my pocked and approached the form with trepidation. I clicked off a couple of shots (one seen here) and scurried on my way. This much I can tell you. . .the form was naked. He was positively anatomically correct. Painted bronze. And frozen in time and space. I have no idea who he was, or what he was doing there in the almost pitch blackness. But I feel his "appearance" had to be sanctioned by the parks department, the city, or some local council on the arts. I tried to speak to him. Ask him a few quick questions – the who, what and all the why's. With little more than the illumination of a few overhead street lamps, people were still strolling by, most on the way to the subway or suburban bus lines, going home from the early night shift. A few individuals walked directly by the stoned man and didn't as much as flinch. Was it only visible to me? Not possible as the pictures I took clearly show. By thinking of Nick Redfern's communication had I somehow created a mystical, phantom, known as a Tulpa in far eastern faiths? Had this stone mime appeared out of nowhere as if to support the ideas and theories espoused in this book?

We may never know, but one thing is certain – to me at least – this has to go down as an unexplained Fortean episode in my life (a term named after writer/researcher Charles Fort who cataloged thousands of incidents of unusual phenomenon).This incident is as strange and unusual as any story you will find in this book, from the giant nicknamed Goliah, to the exceedingly tall UFOnauts sighting in South America as detailed by Scott Corrales, to the anthropoids, giants and mammoths categorized by the late Harold T. Wilkins.

And though we may not be able to identify their true original, we know that giants have always coexisted alongside normal sized humans. Perhaps some have come from an underground world, and others from the heavens. But let us allow logic to take its due course. And so we invite you to suit up in your best armor and prepare to confront whatever may come your way in the land of the mighty and the unexplained.

Timothy Green Beckley, Publisher
MRUFO8@Hotmail.com

The American Goliah

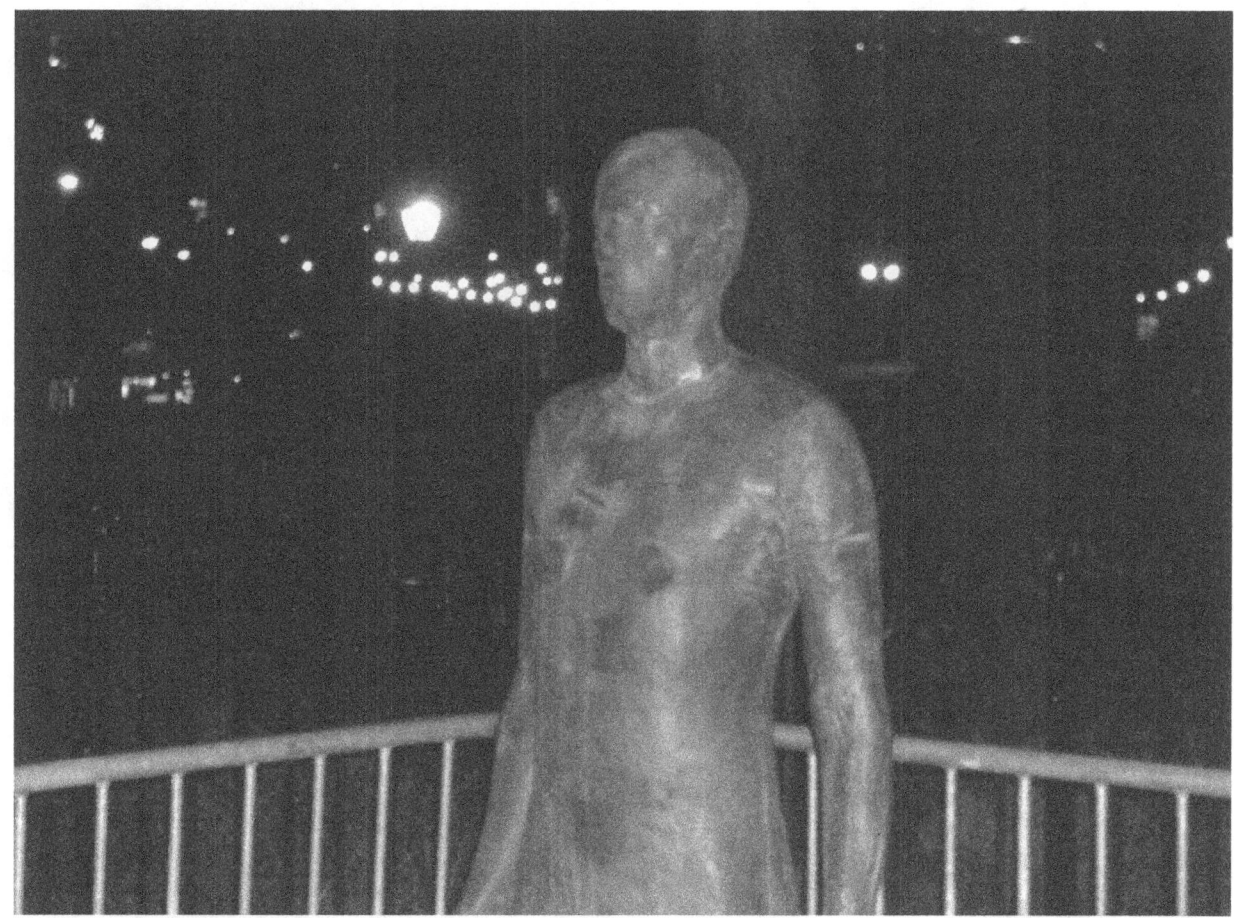

Was this stone-like mime standing at the entrance to Madison Square Park at midnightpart of some weird Tulpa materialization created by the publisher/editor of this book?

The American Goliah

An eminent Orientalist and Biblical scholar, Zecharia Sitchin knows a real anomaly as he stands by one such as this Olmec head.

The Strange Tale of the Cardiff Giant by Nick Redfern

The tale of the legendary Cardiff Giant is just about as weird, as surreal, and as convoluted as any tale can possibly get! And, without doubt, it was one of the most infamous and audacious hoaxes in American history.

Essentially, the giant was nothing less than a 10-foot-tall purported "petrified man," said to have been uncovered on October 16, 1869 by workmen engaged in digging a well behind the barn of one William C. "Stub" Newell in Cardiff, New York.

In reality, however, the giant was nothing of the sort. It was actually the creation of a New York tobacconist named George Hull; an atheist, who decided to create the mighty-form after a heated argument with a fundamentalist minister – a certain Mr. Turk - about the passage in Genesis 6:4 to the effect that giants once roamed the Earth.

Hull's master-plan very quickly came to overwhelming fruition: he secretly hired a group of men to carve the enormous man out of a block of gypsum in Fort Dodge, Iowa, telling them it was intended to be used in the creation of a monument to Abraham Lincoln that would stand proudly in the heart of New York City. When work was complete, Hull shipped the block to Chicago, where he hired a German stone-cutter to further carve it into the likeness of a man – not forgetting, in the process, to swear him to absolute secrecy.

The ruse was a highly ingenious one: a whole variety of stains and acids were used to make the giant appear both ancient and weathered. In addition, the giant's surface was beaten with steel knitting-needles embedded in a board. The purpose: to simulate pores on the skin. If nothing else, Hull had carefully and skillfully thought out his grand-plan.

Then, in November 1868, Hull transported the giant by rail to the farm of his cousin, William Newell. No less than $2,600 was spent on the hoax in total – which was a sizeable amount of money, indeed, way back in the 1860s.

Almost twelve months later, Newell hired Gideon Emmons and Henry Nichols, ostensibly to dig a well, and on October 16, 1869, lo and behold they "found" the Cardiff Giant. One of the men reportedly exclaimed, in excited and exaggerated tones: "I declare: some old Indian has been buried here!"

But that was only the start of the matter: Newell quickly set up a tent over the giant and charged 25-cents for anyone and everyone who wanted to see it. Two days later, very pleased by the huge number of people who turned out to view the Cardiff Giant, he increased the price to 50 cents. Enterprise was truly the name of the game.

Archaeological scholars quickly pronounced the giant nothing more than a fake; while a number of geologists noticed there was no logical reason for digging a well in the exact spot the giant had been found. And Yale palaeontologist Othniel C. Marsh came right to the point, famously declaring the Cardiff Giant a "most decided humbug". There were, however, some gullible Christian fundamentalists and preachers who defended its legitimacy.

Ultimately, Hull sold his part-interest for the very impressive sum of $37,500 to a syndicate of five men headed by one David Hannum. They, then, clandestinely moved the giant form to Syracuse, New York for exhibition. Unsurprisingly, the giant drew such massive crowds that the famous showman P.T. Barnum offered $60,000 for a three-month lease of the giant. When the syndicate flatly turned him down, however, the always-resourceful and industrious Barnum hired a man to create a plaster replica – which quickly went on display in New York, amid claims that this was the real thing, and that the Cardiff Giant was the hoax!

As newspaper journalists gleefully reported on Barnum's version of the story, David Hannum was quoted as saying, "There's a sucker born every minute;" in reference to spectators paying to see Barnum's giant. Over time, the quotation was misattributed to P.T. Barnum himself. Hannum then tried to sue Barnum. In somewhat humorous fashion, however, the judge told Hannum to get his giant to swear on his own genuineness in court if he wanted an injunction in his favor. That was a tough one to achieve.

But still matters were not over: on December 10, Hull confessed the truth to the press. Then, on February 2, 1870 both giants were revealed as fakes in court, and the judge ruled that Barnum could not be sued for calling a fake giant a fake. And that was the end of the lawsuit, not surprisingly.

And the events stirred up something else too: they encouraged others to come forward with their very own versions of the Cardiff Giant. As evidence of this, in 1876 the "Solid Muldoon" surfaced out of Beulah, Colorado and was exhibited at 50 cents a ticket. There was also a rumor going around that Barnum had offered to buy it for $20,000. It was, needless to say, a fake – and possibly one that George Hull himself had a hand in.

One year later, in 1877, the owner of Taughannock House hotel on Cayuga Lake, New York, hired his own merry band of men to create a fake petrified man, and who carefully placed it precisely where the workers that were expanding the hotel would eventually find it. Once again, publicity and public interest were impressive. But, it was still a hoax.

Then, in 1892, a certain Jefferson "Soapy" Smith, the de facto ruler of the town of Creede, Colorado, bought a petrified man – "McGinty," as he became known - for $3,000 and exhibited it for 10 cents a look. Interestingly, this giant was actually real. That's right: a human-body, deliberately injected with chemicals for preservation. Soapy enthusiastically displayed McGinty from 1892 to 1895 throughout Colorado and the northwest United States.

Seven years on – 1899, to be precise - a petrified man was said to have been found in Fort Benton, Montana. The body was supposedly identified as that of U.S. Civil War General Thomas Francis Meagher. Meagher had drowned in the Missouri River two years previously. The petrified man was transported to New York for exhibition; but, needless to say, it was not the general, at all.

The American Goliah

The Cardiff Giant – which started all the fuss – continued to surface from time to time. However, its place in the limelight was clearly waning. In 1901 the giant appeared on display at the Pan-American Exposition, but failed to generate any significant attention or publicity.

Then, some years later, an Iowa-based publisher purchased it – for use as a coffee-table, no less! Seemingly eventually growing tired of the giant, in 1947 the man sold it to the Farmers' Museum in Cooperstown, New York, where it is still on display.

And there's another very good reason why the controversy of the Cardiff Giant refuses to roll over and die.

In January 2010, I gave a lecture at Cooperstown – as part of the Ghosts of Cooperstown event that included presentations from the people behind the History Channel's Ghost Hunters series – on the subject of one of my deep passions: cryyptozoology; which is the search for unknown animals, such as Bigfoot, the Loch Ness Monster and the Chupacabras.

After the lecture, a local woman named Sally came up to me and swore that her father had seen the Cardiff Giant striding through the woods of Cooperstown late one winter's night in 2007. I asked Sally if she was joking. She was not. Her father, Sally said, had been driving home at around 11.00 p.m. one Friday night – after visiting friends in Albany, NY.

As Sally's father approached one particular stretch of road enveloped by trees, he was shocked to the core by the sight of the Cardiff Giant looming out of the woods and striding across the road in several mighty steps. Not surprisingly, he hit the brakes.

Sally told me both she and her father, as locals, had been to see the Cardiff Giant on display at the local museum on several occasions over the years. They also knew full well that it was nothing more than a century-old hoax. So, how could a hoaxed creation be seen wandering the chilled woods of Cooperstown in 2007?

Sally's opinion was that the Cardiff Giant that her father saw was not the same entity that currently rests in the Farmer's Museum. Rather, she felt, he had been blessed with a sighting of a thought-form – a Tulpa – that had been conjured into existence by the sheer unconscious will of those who wished to believe it was real. It was a mind-monster, in other words – one that cannot exist unless people believe in it.

Could it really be the case that a mind-originated Cardiff Giant haunts the darkened parts of Cooperstown, one destined to roam the neighborhood by night, until such a time that a lack of belief in its existence dooms it to inevitable annihilation?

It was as good a theory as any, I suggested. And, as someone who has dug deeply into the world of thought-forms and Tulpas, I reasoned it made a great deal of sense, too.

The saga of the Cardiff Giant, I suspect, is far from over…

****

Nick Redfern is the author of many books on the paranormal, including Contactees; Monsters of Texas; Final Events; and There's something in the Woods. He is a prolific blogger and a frequent guest on such talk shows as Coast to Coast AM, The Para Cast and Joshua Warren's Speaking Of Strange.

This work contains a variety of ideas and theories on the subject of giants and other unexplained humongous creatures as detailed by a number of highly respected researchers in several fields of study.

The following is a reproduction of an original work published well over a century; ago detailing an amazing discovery in upstate New York which remains controversial as does much of the material we are hereby reproducing, much of it for the very first time to a public audience.

The American Goliah

Ancient records indicate that giants were once plentyful.

The Persistence of Giants
by
Scott Corrales

There were giants in the earth in those days.
-- Genesis 6:4

What would the lore of all human cultures be like without the presence of giants? They are a fixture of folktales and myth from Europe and the Americas to the farthest reaches of Asia. They are mentioned with equal ease in holy books and in fairy tales: giants fill us with wonder and not inconsiderable envy as we marvel at their strength and feats. Those dwelling in the Middle Ages, caught in the turbulence of their troubled times, ascribed the engineering achievements of the Roman Empire to the work of giants.

Giants have been relegated to the realms of fable and sword-and-sorcery novels, but there is considerable evidence that beings of great size shared our world in primeval times: Science keeps a low profile when it comes to discussing the existence of large specimens of humanoid life as part of the evolutionary chain, but it is a recognized fact that giant apes existed in the Tertiary period. Olduvai Gorge in Tanzania has produced the jawbones and teeth of massive baboons and other simians. Anthropology and zoology recognize the existence of the Gigantopithecus, which lived some 500,000 years ago in what is today modern China. To judge by other remains of great size, these huge creatures ranged between 10 feet and 13 feet in height. One such colossus whose bones were disinterred in Swartkrans, South Africa, appears to have mastered the use of fire and crafted weapons out of animal bones. Java Man and Aurignacian Man, while hominids, surpass modern humans in height.

The American Goliah
An Uncomfortable Memory

In 1975, Mexico's premier ufologist, Pedro Ferriz, visited the town of Calvillo, Aguascalientes (on the Pacific coast, famous for its intricate mazes of unexplored manmade caves) to inspect some ancient petroglyphs on the property of Víctor Martínez, a local landowner. Martínez told the ufologist that he was ambivalent about the petroglyphs, which he considered unlucky, particularly since "that affair with the giants". When asked to elaborate on what he meant, Martínez explained that he had stumbled upon the ancient skeletons of two extraordinarily large men while tilling the soil. Martínez went into Calvillo to notify the authorities about his find, only to discover that the local police believed him to have killed both giants and wanted to incarcerate him!

The farmer finessed his way out of the predicament, returned to his farm, and set fire to the bones.

The reader may well shake his or her head and mourn the loss of what could have well been the evidence needed to build a watertight case for the existence of giants, but had the bones been delivered to a competent authority, it would not have availed much since human skeletons of larger-than-human size have been disinterred for centuries. The town of Soyopa, in the Mexican state of Sonora, has also yielded evidence of giants. In 1930, a group of laborers clearing out a parcel of land not far from the Yaqui River, allegedly dug up an ancient cemetery that yielded the remains of men with a height in excess of eight feet "buried tier by tier." (New York Times, Dec.2, 1930). Four years later, archaeologist Paxton Hayes would disinter the remains of "a race of giants" in a cave located near Barranca de Cobre (today a national park), only a few hours away from the bustling ports of Los Mochis and Culiacn. French author Robert Charroux discusses similar "undesirable" discoveries being made in the former USSR: a cave in the Caucasus presented explorers with the remains measuring between 9'2 and 9'10.

The Bible (considered by many as the default auctoritas in these matters) features a number of highly interesting incidents involving giants. In the Book of Numbers, a party of scouts sent out by Moses to reconnoiter the land of Canaan reach Hebron (a prominent location in recent UFO lore) and learn that the "descendants of Anak" live in the region. They return to their leader, informing him that the region they had been sent to explore was occupied by giants. The Book of Deuteronomy abounds on this, speaking of the great cities with massive earthworks and ramparts, built by the Anakim. Other beings of great stature (in excess of 9-10 ft.) are mentioned in the Scriptures, such as the fearsome warrior Goliath and Og, the King of Bashan. Some Hebraic and Muslim sources also suggest that Adam himself was a giant.

Yet mention of the Biblical giants is not circumscribed to the Pentateuch: 2 Samuel 21:19 mentions a war against the enigmatic Philistines and the slaying of four giant warriors by Elhanan and other Jewish fighters. We are told that the giants "had twelve fingers on their hands and twelve toes on their feet" and that the foursome "were descended from the giants in Gat." This feat is reiterated in 1 Chronicles 20:4-8, which discusses the campaigns of David against his enemies: "...Sibecai slew Sipai, of the descendants of the giants...and Elhanan son of Jair slew Lahmi, brother of Goliath, whose spear was as big as a weaver's beam...these were the descendants of the giants in Gat."

In his book Atlantis and the Giants (Faber,1952), Denis Saurat makes an interesting observation pertaining to the Vulgate Bible (the earliest translation of the scriptures into Latin). The book of Baruch goes over the subject of giants once more, this time in greater detail: "There were giants born that were famous of old, great of stature and expert in war. These did not God choose, neither gave he the way of knowledge unto them -- hence they all perished."

Nineteenth century sources, which have been quoted to exhaustion in countless books and magazines, point to a great number of archaeological finds which involve the presence of human bones of great size. One such find in Greece produced not one but two gigantic skeletons, measuring 34 feet (London Mirror, Jan.11, 1840). In all likelihood, the awestruck discoverers must have come across the remains of some large prehistoric mammal, but the same argument cannot be made for the sizeable tools and weapons which have also been unearthed over the course of centuries. In his book Worlds Before Our Own (Berkeley, 1978) author Brad Steiger reports the discovery of a copper axe weighing 38 pounds at a burial mound in the American Midwest. It would be impossible for any normal-sized warrior, no matter how strong, to wield such a heavy weapon.

Hans Bellamy invoked the force exerted by Earth's moon to account for the existence of giants in our planet's past, and also to explain the construction of cyclopean structures found around the world from South America to the Syrian Desert. Citing the disturbing theories of Austrian thinker Hans Horebiger, Denis Saurat suggested that 300,000 years ago, in the midst of the Pleistocene, the moon was far closer to our planet than it is today and the seas were unimaginably deep. Atmospheric pressure, Saurat argued, was considerably lower, and a race of giants emerged. These tall creatures aided and abetted the development of homo sapiens. It is immediately apparent how such a theory could be disquieting to establishment researchers.

The Codexes Speak

Latin American sources are quite prolix on the subject of giants, to the extent that a number of anthropologists are tempted to consider them the original civilization of Mesoamerica, much to the dismay of their colleagues.

Fernando Alva Ixtlilxochitl, one of the early chroniclers of Mexico's history, mentions in his book Obras Histǿricas the widespread belief that the Chichimecs, the earliest occupants of what is now Mexico, had to displace an old race of giants that lived there (echoes not only of the Bible, but of early legends surrounding the elimination of giants from Britain by a Trojan warrior named Brutus), thus accounting for the persistent discovery of abnormally large remains. Ixtlilxochitl mentions the strife between the giants known as Quinametzin and normal-sixed humans.

Memory of the Quinametzin was widespread throughout Mesoamerica, as evidenced by information gleaned by Spanish explorers and colonizers. Bernal Diaz del Castillo, who accompanied Cortez on his conquest of the Aztec Empire, wrote of a belief among the Tlaxcalan people that "...their ancestors had shared the land with men and women of very tall bodies and large bones, and since they were very wicked and ill mannered, [the ancestors] slew them in combat, and what remained of them died out...".

The American Goliath

The information turned up by early missionaries is also quite intriguing. Fray Diego Durán claimed to have seen the bones "of immense giants" excavated "out of rough places". Fray Gerónimo de Mendieta was told by the older natives that their predecessors had been forced to struggle against giants, "and after this land was won, the bones of many tall men were found." Bernardo de Sahagún, the great Franciscan missionary, would be the first to suggest that the pyramids of Teothihuacan and Cholula were the handiwork of the vanished giant race. Wherever the conquistadors went, more stories were added to the body of information concerning these creatures. When the rapacious Nuno de Guzman reached what is today Jalisco, he demanded to know from the natives why a number of towns had been abandoned. They informed him that the towns had been inhabited by a band of giants who had come up from the south.

Eighteenth century scholars such as Francisco Javier Clavijero were convinced that Mexico's early occupants had indeed been creatures of above average height, judging by the sheer number of remains found (which have apparently not survived to our time).

There was to be no peaceful co-existence between the Quinametzin and the newly-arrived humans, who called them quinametzin hueytlacame ("huge deformed men" or "monstrous giants"). The advancing human tribes (tentatively identified as Olmecs and Toltecs) drove the giants out of their ancestral domain, causing some of them to flee to the north and others to the south, following the Pacific coastline down to Central America. Fray Jos, Mariano Rothea, a Jesuit, sums up this belief as follows: "...in very ancient times there came men and women of extraordinary height, seemingly in flight from the North. Some of them went along the coast of the Southern Sea, while others took to the rough mountainsides..."

Fray Andr,s de Olmos, writing in the 16th century, mentions a curious detail: the Mexican giants nourished themselves on oak acorns and a variety of weeds. This detail contained in the codexes enables us to contemplate a strange possibility: could the Quinametzin have survived into our present age under the guise of the tall, hirsute simian beings known as Bigfoot, Yeti, Sasquatch and myriad other denominations? Those interviewed by the Colonial-era chroniclers explained that tradition held that those giants who were not exterminated by normal-sized humans were chased into the wilderness, where remnants of their race still endure. Marc Dem, the French author of a number of works on the paranormal, has identified the Biblical "Anakim" with giant beings such as the Asian Yeti.

Aztec religious texts such as the Annals of Cuautitl n, which contains the now-famous "Legend of the Five Suns", make mention of the giants, who lived in a distant age of mankind ruled by the second of the five suns ("Taltonatiuh"). The destruction of the giants came about when "jaguars" swept out of the night to devour them all out of existence. Contemporary scholarship tells us that there was nothing at all paranormal about the rampaging felines that destroyed the giants -- the were merely Olmec warriors bearing the jaguar motif on their weapons.

Giants of the South

Giant lore is not exclusive to Mexico. Their considerably large footprints lead us from Mesoamerica into South America itself, where another Spanish priest collected a slightly more chilling account from the native occupants of what is today modern Ecuador.

Pedro Cieza de Le¢n, a chaplain who accompanied the handful of Spaniards who managed to overthrow the powerful Inca Empire in the 1500's, collected a curious and highly significant piece of information concerning giants: the natives had been astonished and terrified to see a reed raft arrive on their shores bearing a shipload of beings "so tall that from the knee down they were as big as the full length of an ordinary fair-sized man..." There was nothing gentle about these giants: Cieza's informants described them as having a hideous appearance, clad in animal skins or naked, and bent on raping and murdering. Could this band of pillagers have formed part of the southward migration of giants described in the Mexican chronicles compiled by the Jesuit Rothea? Zechariah Sitchin's The Lost Realms (Avon,1990) echoes this account in the chronicles collected by Fernando Montesinos, a Spanish visitor to Per£, who mentioned an old Inca tradition describing the colonization of the Peruvian coastal plain by "men of great stature" equipped with metal tools. The depredations of these giants ended when a "heavenly fire" consumed them all.

The American Goliah

In any event, the existence of cyclopean ruins in the southern Americas would indicate the possibility that earlier colossi -- unrelated to the marauding Quinametzin -- applied themselves to the task of creating the massive stonework found in Perú, Bolivia, Chile and even in Brazil. While ruins of great antiquity such as Bolivia's Tiahuanaco appeared to have been built for creatures of a standard height, other structures such as Chile's El Enladrillado give the impression of having been crafted by and for giants. This expansive stadium or amphitheatre, located at an altitude well in excess of 5000 feet near Alto de Vilches in northern Chile, boasts square-cut stone blocks some 16 feet tall and 26 feet long. The manner in which these formidable construction materials were hauled across the precipices of the Andes to a such a high-altitude location defies speculation. El Enladrillado also boasts a track half a mile long by two hundred feet wide, made up of 233 colossal stone blocks, each with an estimated weight of 22,000 pounds.

Such architectural oddities do not automatically make the case for the existence of giants: many ancient monarchies sought to impress and terrify their subjects with buildings on a grandiose scale. A good example is a monumental statue of Constantine the Great, sculpted around 320 A.D., which must have soared thirty feet into the air. All that remains of this colossus today is its 8 foot tall head. Although invoking extraterrestrial aid in their construction was popular for a while, we are still faced with ancient lore stating that giants were employed as skilled labor in the construction of such sites. We can find this not only in South America but also in classical sources which the reader may find more familiar, such as The Odyssey. Greek tradition ascribed the construction of numerous structures to these one-eyed giants.

Mad About Mu

Any discussion of the role of giant-lore in cryptoarchaeology would be incomplete without mentioning, at least in passing, the Lemurian giants conjured up by Helena Petrovna Blavatsky, the guiding light of the Theosophical movement at the turn of the last century.

One can make the lighthearted observation that Lemuria -- or Mu -- plays Avis to Atlantis' Hertz: the second best, "we try harder" lost continent. The lack of classical sources with regard to the lost continent of the Pacific Ocean has made Mu a convenient canvas upon which all manner of speculation can be depicted.

According to Madame Blavatsky, the giant Lemurians stood some 10 to 15 feet tall, had skins resembling alligator hide, faces with protuberant mandibles, small eyes on the sides of their skulls, and elongated, double-jointed limbs. By her description, Mu was a far cry from the halcyon Atlantis: it was a barren land covered in the emanations of active volcanoes, which caused its colossal inhabitants to live in crude huts made of hardened lava. But Mme. Blavatsky improved her creations' lot considerably by adding that with the passing of aeons, these towering monsters evolved into the ancestors of the Australian aborigines and other Melanesian peoples (the racist implications of this idea are self-evident).

Could there be a grain of truth, however, in Blavatsky's fantasy? Most traditions, even Biblical ones, imply that there was no kinship between humans and the giant race. Could a "lost continent" such as Lemuria, Mu or the Gondwana favored by the paleogeologists, have hosted the separate development of a race of giants?

French scholar M.P. Millet, an adherent of the concept of polygenesis, supported the existence of a number of hominid phyla: one of them, which emigrated from Africa into Asia, included Sinanthropus, Gigantopithecus and Meganthropus. This branch of hominidae disappeared. The second phylum remained in Africa and consists of Parenthropus and Plesianthropus, who spanned the globe and had an average height of 6.5' to 9 feet.

Venturing once more into speculation, we could say that prehistoric hominids whose remains have been found in Java and in Asia (Sinanthropus and Gigantopithecus) developed rudimentary cultures that spread across the Pacific and into the Americas (if not globally), giving rise not only to the Quinametzin and South American giants who allegedly assisted in the construction of Tiahuanaco, but accounting for the giant man-apes of the North American Pacific region. Modern anthropology texts no longer include Gigantopithecus among the protohumans, having relegated it to the category of giant monkey.

Conclusion

Delving into the twin subjects of cryptoarchaeology and cryptoantrhopology is to rush into a briar patch of controversial and often conflicting information -- a minefield that can inflict considerable damage to the researcher, no matter how honest his or her intentions. Much of this "revisionist" information -- as it is despectively known by the scientific community -- has been made to serve the purposes of racial bigotry (Blavatsky), creationistic doctrines (as in the case of the human footprints of the Paluxy River) and even Nazism (Adolf Hitler and his followers were faithful disciples of Hans Horebiger's theory of evolution/devolution, using it as ammunition to support their quest for the "master race"). Discussion of the countless anomalies which have filled many a book over the past five or six decades can, in some instances, create the impression that the researcher is trying to further one of the aforementioned doctrines, which could not be farther from the truth.

Establishment scientist and academics look upon these anomalies with considerable irritation, charging that the giant bones found often belong to early mammals (which is true in many cases) and that the dating methods used were either improperly applied or not used at all -- which puts paid, in their viewpoint, to any discrepancies in age. But the dating methods employed by anthropology and archaeology are hardly foolproof: fluorine dating, for example, provides only a relative age and does not operate in tropical regions of the planet or regions which were once upon a time tropical (such as Antarctica); Carbon-14 dating, which has been the workhorse of field since its inception, is useful in dating organic items for no period earlier than eleven thousand years ago; uranium series dating, amino-acid racemigation (which is subject to contamination, as with all organic dating procedures) and thermoluminesence have in many cases yielded dates much older than expected.

The debate over the existence of giants in prehistoric and historic times will probably never be satisfactorily resolved. Neither side will convince the other that it is in sole possession of the truth. However, to quote Denis Saurat: "And what indeed is Truth if not that which men have always believed in?"

Off the wind swept coast of Easter Island tall figures
stand perhaps as a representation of those who once visited this remote land.

South American Giant Ufonauts
by
Scott Corrales

News of an alleged three-meter-tall non-human entity shambling toward a roadside in Chile (March 2010) brought back memories of the truly giant UFO occupants that were commonly reported in the 1950s and '60s, usually in Argentina, Brazil and Chile, although cases in Spain and even the USA were reported. As with everything involving UFOs, we must first assume good faith on the part of people who are beyond our reach: the witness, the magazine or newspaper in which the story first appeared, and so forth. These cases were made known to U.S. audiences by Jim and Coral Lorenzen's books on UFOs in the Sixties and Seventies, contributed by a formidable network of correspondents and advisors in other countries. Some reports suggested that their tall stature proved beyond question their non-terrestrial origin, as even humans who will someday be born in a low-gravity environment may attain considerable height. Their purposes seemed centered on "gathering samples", much like their other occupants reported at the time, or sometimes chasing terrified witnesses (potential "samples"? Who knows) who made narrow escapes.

An argument can be made in the recent Chilean sighting that energy released in tremendous earthquakes may cause unusual effects in the human mind, perhaps leading individuals to see what isn't there, or misinterpret what they're seeing. But it is nonetheless worth looking back at some of the cases that we have accumulated over the decades before relegating giant UFO-related beings to the company of the Jolly Green Giant.

An Argentinean Giant

In January 2002, Argentinean researcher Pablo Omastott brought the following case to the attention of Quique Mario, director of that country's Proyecto Condor UFO research group. The event, a CE-III involving a motorcyclist and a giant entity, had appeared in the January 15 issue of the Córdoba newspaper.

Enrique Moreno, 19, a clerical employee with the Ika-Renault corporation whose nocturnal job involves acting as a courier for business documents from one company office to another. Arriving at one of Ika-Renault's offices in the dark of the night to lay some paperwork in the middle of a table, he realized that the facility's lights flickered on and off inexplicably. Moreno paid no mind to the power fluctuation and hopped on his motorcycle, heading for his next destination.

Upon reaching a site where vehicles were parked before being sent out across the Andes to Chile, Moreno was amazed to see a giant green figure some 150 meters away. Thinking at first that it might be a welder carrying out his duties at that time of the night, the courier got on his motorcycle and drove toward the figure. When he came within thirty meters, his otherwise dependable bike backfired and hesitated, shuddering and becoming almost unmanageable. Moreno had to perform extraordinary efforts to remain in control of his two-wheeler, but he was much more distressed by the glowing figure than by his vehicle's unaccustomed reaction.

"I froze after seeing it," said Moreno. "It was like a robot standing more than two meters tall. Its angled head was hairless, it had shining, luminous eyes, and was dressed like a frogman, wearing a belt with a wide oval buckle around its waist."

The ungovernable motorcycle shot like an arrow out of control crossing an open gate and going straight across the road without its driver being able do a single thing about it.

"My arms still ache; it robbed me of my strength," he told the interviewer from Córdoba. "I felt as though I was in the middle of a magnetic field. It was cold that night, but the area surrounding me was very hot."

After the experience, Moreno stumbled through the factory's gates feeling a terrible buzzing in his head, as though it were about to explode. Factory personnel immediately drove him to a clinic where he was given sedatives. Although the newspaper considers that the young courier may have hallucinated the experience, it adds that there were other witnesses to the entity that very same evening: a nurse at the same medical facility Moreno had been driven to had administered a sedative to a woman who claimed having seen the same colossal figure levitate through the air and enter an unidentified flying object--an event which was confirmed, in turn, by residents of Villa de El Libertador, who had seen the alleged spacecraft that same evening.

As if these corroborating accounts were not enough, there is also the case involving trucker Luftolde Rodríguez, 52, who was slowly turning his tractor-trailer around and was terrified to find the green giant standing in front of his rig. The giant's presence appeared to drain not only the vehicle's power source, but the trucker's wristwatch and portable radio as well.

Given his proximity to the unknown figure, Rodríguez was better able to describe it. The giant, he said, was looking at him inquisitively; it had a flattened head, was completely bald and lacked eyebrows and eyelashes. Its ears were long, and it wore a glowing light blue outfit with a broad black belt and white boots. An interesting detail is that Rodríguez reports that the giant had a ball "similar to a billiard ball" in its left hand.

The article in Córdoba offers the following conclusion: "The giant's attitude was entirely harmless and could be said to be one of observation. The entity was completely made of energy, perhaps belonging to a form of life in which protoplasm no longer plays any part."

"Tallfellows" and Truck Drivers

Much has been written about people's love for their automobiles. Given the number of cars on our roads, the fact is unquestionable. However, not much has been put down on paper regarding the UFO phenomenon's similar affection for the humble car. Prior to the age of abductions, a fair share of UFO cases involved unsuspecting motorists.

"RV" never suspected he would be one of them.

As he drove at three o'clock in the morning along Spain's A-68 highway from the city of Logroño back to his home in the Basque country, the anonymous protagonist of our story was more interested in pulling into the nearest rest area rather than having a close encounter with the unknown. As luck would have it, he found one such rest stop further along the road, deserted but for the presence of large French tractor-trailer whose driver had obviously had the same idea.

"RV" parked his Citroen BX, turned off the ignition, and promptly shut his eyes, drifting off to sleep before he even knew it. Despite being a sound sleeper, "RV" was wakened by a slight buzzing sound and a bright light which he at first thought to come from another vehicle--perhaps another articulated trailer--pulling into the rest stop. The bright light gradually dimmed to extinction, and early morning darkness reigned over the area once more.

Even as he reflected on the sudden burst of light's origin, "RV" saw the driver of the French tractor-trailer exit the cab of his vehicle and approach the car with great urgency, pointing at the empty field adjacent to the rest area. "Did you see that?" asked the trucker in French.

"RV" cautiously got out of his car and was stunned. The source of the unexpected brightness turned out to be a vast dark structure, blacker than the surrounding night. The French trucker brimmed over with fear and nervous excitement, but willingly followed "RV"'s lead toward the dark structure.

When interviewed by Spanish ufologist Juan José Benítez in 1988, the year the event had occurred, "RV" could not explain what had possessed him to take the lead in a potentially foolhardy excursion, and he admitted to "not being a very curious person." Both men walked an estimated ten meters toward the ominous object before running into what can best be described as an "invisible wall". RV's eyeglasses pressed against his face as he hit the strange barrier, which he would describe to Benítez as having a gelatinous or plastic consistency. Even scarier was the green luminescence which emerged from nowhere to outline the looming dark structure.

The French trucker vented a few choice expletives in his language, which caused RV to take a second look at the structure with the greenish cast: twin colossi had seemingly emerged from the vehicle, advancing slowly toward the humans. Knees trembling with fear, RV guessed their height at three meters (9.8 feet), and their width seemed to match.

During the interview, RV was careful to state that he did not believe the colossi were robots--at least not mechanicals as we've come to understand them. They moved in unison, "as though they were reflections of one another." Their faces were featureless, their arms hung by their sides, and their massive legs appeared to be slightly articulated. Silent in the darkness, the pair of giants stared impassively at the two humans at a distance of five meters. Whatever courage or curiosity the truck driver and RV may have felt evaporated: both men broke into a frantic run, eventually hiding behind RV's car.

The entire event, which lasted about an hour, ended with a very slight buzzing sound coming from the dark structure, which began moving away at low altitude before disappearing. RV guessed that the structure could have conceivably been a hundred meters in diameter (roughly three hundred feet) and never once thought that the object and its silent "crew" could have been the product of any Earth technology. "Any country that has access to such artifacts will dominate the planet at its leisure," he told Benítez.

But the details surrounding the brush with the unknown were event stranger: during the entire hour, not a single car or truck had driven past the rest area in spite of the fact that the A-68 highway is a major artery; the French trucker jumped aboard his rig and "put the hammer down", zooming away from the rest area at top speed, not even bothering to exchange notes with RV regarding the bizarre occurrence both had shared. The battery of RV's Citroen BX became unable to hold a charge, despite the fact that the car was only a year old. Strange blister-like deformities appeared on the rear windshield and the front bumper, the parts of the Citroen which were made of plastic. Mechanics attributed them to proximity to a heat source. Nor did magnetic media fare much better: RV's credit cards refused to work at automatic teller machines.

Researcher Benítez was not disappointed when he visited the rest area in search of physical evidence. Only a short distance away from the blacktopped parking lot he found a large swath of grassy terrain that looked bleached and broken in comparison with the surroundings--desiccated without showing signs of having been singed or burned.

Giants, Guards and Gunfire

In the fateful early morning hours of that November day twenty six years ago, around 2:45 a.m., José María Trejo and Juan Carriozosa were standing guard outside the air base's fuel depot, each in their own guard shack, separated by a distance of two hundred feet. The night, which had otherwise been uneventful, was shattered by a loud, piercing, whistling sound that caused the soldiers to cover their ears for about five minutes. The high-pitched noise ended abruptly, causing the soldiers to emerge from their shacks. Given that they were insuring the safety of tens of thousands of gallons of jet fuel, the possibility of a terrorist attack crossed their minds.

Armed with submachine guns, the soldiers decided to comb the area beyond Trejo's guard shack, which seemed to be closer to the source of the sound. They had only advanced a few feet when the high-pitched whistling sound was heard again, loud enough "to drive us crazy," in Carrizosa's words. Things were only getting started.

The very moment the second whistle-blast ended, the sky became filled with an intense light, "brighter than a flare", which lasted some twenty seconds. Both soldiers were amazed at the unsuspected display, and were still exchanging questions about it when a third soldier joined them, asking if they'd seen the light. Deciding that these events were a bit too unsettling not to be reported, they summoned the duty corporal, who ordered the three soldiers and a guard dog--a wolf hybrid--to patrol the area and check for anything unusual.

A crackling sound arose unexpectedly from a eucalyptus tree. The soldiers unleashed their growling dog, which ran at top speed toward the darkened area. The three men held their submachine guns tightly, expecting to hear the guard dog barking at an intruder. "The wolf-dog came back to us," Trejo told researcher García, "but it seemed dazed, dizzy, as though someone or something had given it a beating or frightened it out of its wits."

The American Goliah

The three soldiers began shouting challenges into the darkness, fingers on their triggers, expecting at any moment to find themselves in a heated gun-battle with intruders bent on detonating the fuel depot.

"I felt a strange sensation," reported Trejo. "Something was standing behind me. Out of the corner of my eye I could see a green light. Spinning around on a heel, I found myself faced with the most fantastic and inexplicable sight I could've envisioned: a nine-foot tall human figure made of green light."

Even stranger, remarked another of the witnesses, was that the figure appeared to be composed of small points of green light, giving it a small head, thick torso and extremely long arms. The luminous giant appeared to have neither legs nor feet.

Trejo tried to fire a hail of bullets at the figure, but found it impossible to pull his Z-62 submachine gun's trigger. Indeed, a gradual stiffening was taking over his body, inducing a sensation of lassitude. He could see and hear perfectly, however, managing to shout: "Get down, they're killing us!" before hitting the ground face first.

Trejo's terrified brothers-in-arms were not stricken by the enigmatic paralysis and opened fire against the towering green figure, estimating a total of forty or fifty shots between them. The green giant became brighter, "like the flash of a picture camera" before fading like an image on a television screen.

Talavera de la Real was in turmoil. Alarms were sounded as some soldiers took up defensive positions and others headed for the fuel depot. The three sentries were hard pressed to explain what had occurred to an irate superior officer. But what saved them from an uncomfortable stay in the base's stockade was a cold physical fact: despite having ordered fifty men to comb the area in broad daylight, not a single cartridge case was found. A masonry wall behind the place where the green giant materialized should have been pockmarked with bullet impacts, but was otherwise intact.

But it was Trejo--the first one to see the green intruder--who would pay the price physically: only a few days after the incident, he was afflicted by sudden bouts of blindness to which neither the

Giants of Andalusia

Happening upon giant beings engaged in bizarre activities is bad enough; being pursued by them is a veritable nightmare.

Andrés Gómez Serrano, a retired Spanish police officer turned UFO researcher, has been aided by his years of being in uniform in getting to the bottom of a number of UFO and paranormal mysteries that have occurred with a certain degree of frequency on his "beat" -- the Spanish cities of Algeciras and Cádiz. The result of his work has been collected in the book OVNIS: 50 Años de Investigación en el Campo de Gibraltar (Antakara, 2000).

For reasons unknown, this section of the Iberian peninsula is rife with sightings involving giant entities associated with enigmatic craft, but none of them quite matches the hair-raising events of February 1980.

On the 6th of that month, following a spate of nocturnal light sightings in the vicinity of Botafuegos, three children decided to take it upon themselves to investigate the possible landing of one of the lights--described as a giant "Ferris wheel" -- along the road leading from Botafuegos to the town of El Cobre. The three youngsters, like characters out of a Spielberg movie, equipped themselves with a little more than flashlights and set off on their adventure. Upon crossing a stream which had to be forded in order to reach their goal, something unusual occurred: their flashlights, powered by fresh batteries, suddenly went out. When they decided to return to their starting point, the portable light sources regained their power. Startled, the children crossed the invisible barrier several times, noticing the same inexplicable power loss on each occasion. Unable to explain the oddity, the children returned home.

The nocturnal light show continued unabated. On the night of February 11th, as the three children witnessed "their light" make what appeared to be a zigzag landing on the slopes of the nearby hills, a car driven by Rafael Tobaja and his wife pulled up to them. Tobaja asked: "Did you just see the same thing my wife and I saw back in San Jose Artesano?" When the youngsters assented, Tobaja told them to hop in the back seat, and drove them to find the strange object.

At 9:45 p.m., Tobaja and his passengers reached the gates of a farm known as "La Rejanosa". Getting out of the car to check the surroundings, the group was startled by an enormous white light that slowly rose from behind a low hill, splitting in two. From each luminous half there emerged a gigantic, man-shaped entity, with elongated legs and arms, standing in excess of nine feet tall. The radiance of their bodies made it impossible to make out their faces.

The humans stared bemusedly at the luminous giants until they realized the entities were heading straight toward them.

Fear gripped Mrs. Tobaja, whose panicked screams added to the hair-scene. Clearly aware of the danger, and of his liability in having brought three unknown children into the perilous situation, Rafael Tobaja overcame his fear-induced paralysis and shouted: "Back in the car! Everybody get in the car!"

Had the unreal event been a scene from a movie screenplay, the engine in Tobaja's car would not have turned over, exacerbating panic to unspeakable heights. But the coupe started normally and the driver pulled away from the luminous giants at full speed, not stopping to look back until he had reached the neighborhood where his young passengers --badly shaken companions in adventure -- resided.

The following day, researcher Gómez visited "La Rejanosa" in the company of Manuel Aguilar, a local surveyor and engineer, to reconnoiter the premises. Both men found a profusion of triangular "boot marks" on the ground and an impression left by an object of considerable weight. Inquiries made of the military suggested that the triangular marks may have been left by mortars during live-fire exercises; however, no maneuvers had been conducted during that week in February or even earlier.

Making Sense of it All...

Giant UFO occupants have not formed part of recent case histories, and especially not during the abduction-haunted 1990's. They appear to be confined to certain parts of the world, as though assigned to them. Very few of them have taken place in the United

The American Goliah

States, and the only one worthy of mention is the August 1973 incident which occurred in Buffalo Mills, Pennsylvania, were residents saw a 9 foot tall giant with "a baleful expression" as it walked down the main street.

During the early days of ufology, speculation had it that the giant ufonauts were bred to perform a specific task, just as the small, large-headed ones seemed to be good at certain others. In the Botafuego case, the giants appeared insubstantial--projections designed to frighten away notoriously curious humans, perhaps? Had the entities been bent on enforcing a "no witnesses" policy, they could have surely caught up with the escaping vehicle in a few bounds. In the Talavera del Real case, we again find another insubstantial giant seemingly "probing the defenses" of a military facility.

The concept of these giants as security measures is highlighted in the case involving "RV" and the French trucker at the rest area. Were the monoliths involved in guarding a massive craft--probably a mothership--that made a provisional landing for unknown reasons?

Some of those who believe earth was visited in the past by ancient astronauts have been able to offer up visual evidence that large sized beings literally made slaves of humans such as the case of this Sumerian Giant King.

The American Goliah
by Anon.

AN ANCIENT HUMAN GIANT OR A HUNDRED YEAR OLD HOAX?

1869

The American Goliah

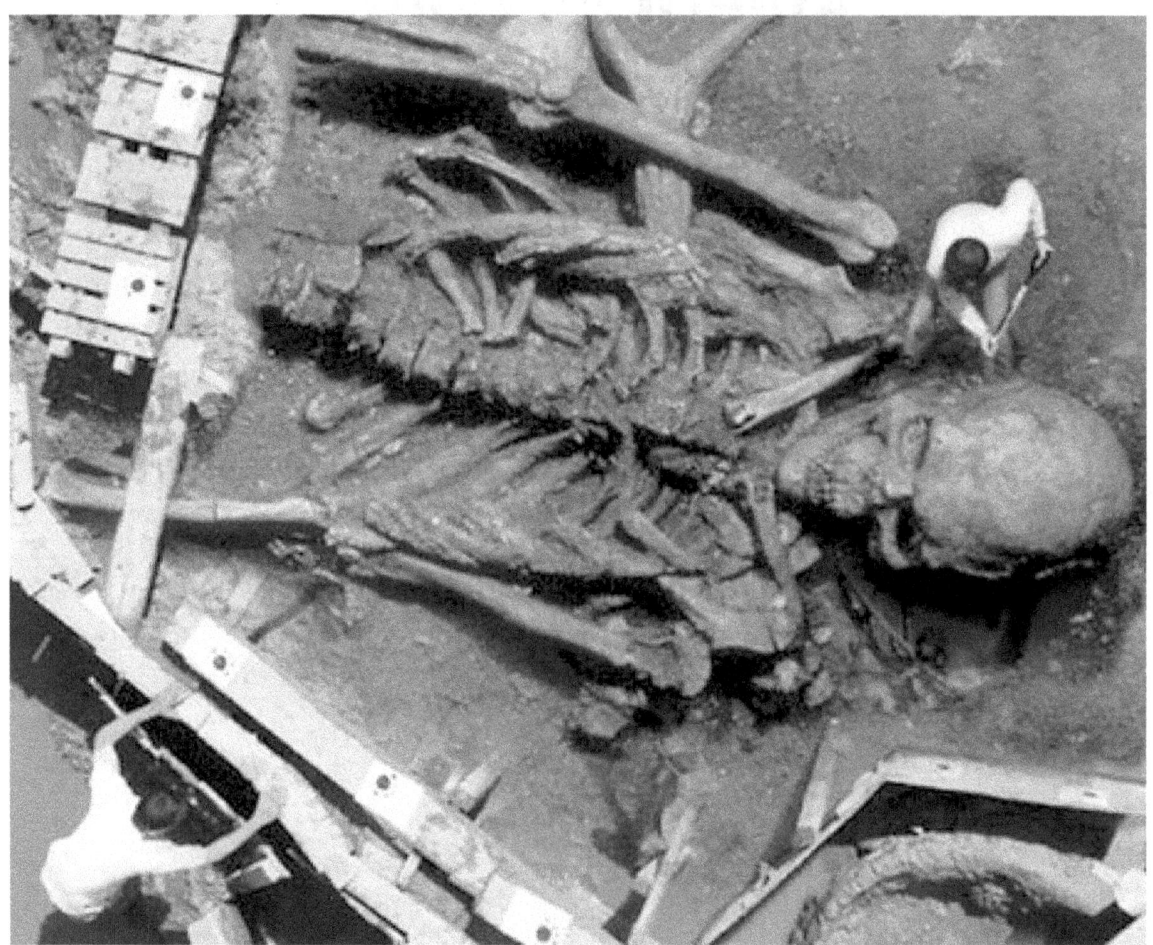

Remains of gigantic beings have surfaced over the decades, but they often go missing as the archaeological community tries to defuse the existence of such human and not so human abnormalities.

The American Goliah

THE AMERICAN GOLIAH.

A WONDERFUL GEOLOGICAL DISCOVERY.

A PETRIFIED GIANT,

TEN AND ONE-HALF FEET HIGH, DISCOVERED IN ONONDAGA COUNTY, N. Y.

HISTORY OF THE DISCOVERY ON OCTOBER 16, 1869, OF AN IMAGE OF STONE, THE SAME BEING A PERFECTLY FORMED AND WELL DEVELOPED MAN. DESCRIPTIONS OF THE PETRIFACTION, WITH

The Opinions of Scientific Men Thereon.

1869.

The American Goliah

The American Goliah
A Wonderful Geological Discovery

A PETRIFIED GIANT Ten And One-Half Feet High Discovered In Onondaga County, N.Y.

History of the discovery on October 16, 1869, of an image of stone, the same being a perfectly formed and well developed man, descriptions of the petrification, with the opinions of scientific men thereon.

SPECIAL NOTICE

This pamphlet is the only authorized account of the discovery of the great wonder and the latest facts regarding management; and is the only publication furnished by the owners of the Giant with immediate and authentic information of any examinations, experiments or new developments regarding it. Such new facts will be immediately added to this pamphlet, together with such scientific opinions as may be of interest or value to the public.

The statements herein contained have been taken from the lips of living witnesses on the ground where the events transpired, (excepting where reports are credited to other sources,) and can be depended upon as reliable.

This publication will be found valuable for preservation, as it records perhaps the most important scientific discovery of this century. Certainly the wonder is something that in the whole history of this country has never been exceeded, even if ever equaled.

This pamphlet combines all the important facts as narrated by the newspaper press, in addition to whatever others may occur, placing them in a convenient form for permanent preservation.

Wonderful Scientific Discovery.
A Giant Of Stone

10 1-2 Feet High, Exhumed In Onondaga County, N.Y.

On Saturday forenoon, Oct. 16th, 1869, William C. Newell, a farmer residing near the village of Cardiff, in the town of Lafayette, County of Onondaga, commenced to dig a well near his barn. Two workmen were employed, Gideon Emmons and Henry Nichols; Mr. Newell being engaged meanwhile in drawing stone with which to line the well. At the depth of about three feet one of the workmen struck a stone, as he at first supposed. A moment later he thought it a water lime pipe, and asked for an ax with which to break it. Before the ax arrived the foot was partially uncovered, with the exclamation, "I declare, some old Indian has been buried here!" Farther excavation disclosed the entire foot, and a part of the leg. One of the workmen, seeing the direction in which the body lay, dug down just above where he thought the head might be, and his shovel struck the nose. The face and head were soon uncovered, and in a short time the entire figure exposed to view. There then appeared to the few assembled spectators the colossal, well-proportioned form of a human being of the following remarkable DIMENSIONS.

From top of head to instep of sole, ten feet three inches. If standing in a perfectly upright position, the height would be ten feet, seven or eight inches.

The American Goliah

Length of head from chin to top of head, twenty-one inches.

Nose, from brow to tip, six inches--across base of nostrils, three and one-half inches.

Mouth four inches.

Shoulders from point to point, three feet.

Circumference of neck thirty-seven inches.

Length of right arm from point of shoulder to end of middle finger, four feet, nine and one-half inches.

Across palm of hand, seven inches.

Length of second finger from knuckle joint, eight inches.

Across wrist, five inches. Distance around thighs, (about half way between knee and thigh joints,) five feet, seven and one-half inches.

Leg, from hip joint to knee joint, three feet; through thigh, one foot; through calf, nine and one-half inches.

Foot, nineteen and one-half inches.

The discovery, as may be supposed, created an immense sensation. Mr. Newell was much perplexed and annoyed and determined at one time to fill up the excavation and keep the discovery from the knowledge of the public. Some years ago a razor was found in a hollow stump near by and suspicions were then thrown out that a murder had been committed. The family feared that the corpse of the murdered man would in some manner confront them through this discovery.

A rush occurred of neighbors and others to see the exhumed wonder, for intelligence of the Giant spread on the wings of the wind. The excitement and ceaseless questions still farther confused the mind of the quiet proprietor and he almost unconsciously consented to various suggestions. One was that the body be raised that day (Saturday,)--consent for which Mr. Newell acknowledges to have given. Ropes were procured and preparations made therefor, but the lateness of the afternoon hour caused its postponement. This is a matter of rejoicing to scientific men, as well as the public generally; for every one naturally wishes to see the Giant as he had slept in his bed for centuries, and for themselves examine the winding sheets he wrapped about him.

Position of the Figure.

The form is lying on its back, the head towards the east and the feet toward the west. The reclining posture is a perfectly natural one, the limbs and feet being slightly drawn up. The figure appears as if a person had fallen there and died. There seem to be evidences of considerable physical anguish in the position of the limbs, of the body, and in the tension of the nerves as well as the contraction of the muscles (which are fully developed.) The right hand rests upon the lower abdomen, and the left is pressed against the back directly opposite. The left foot is thrown partially over the right one, the leg resting partly upon its fellow, but not crossing it. The head is inclined to the right.

The face is the only part seemingly free from traces of the agony of dissolution. The expression is calm, thoughtful, almost sweet. The high, massive forehead sets off with grand, yet benevolent dignity, the well rounded and proportioned features. The countenance is a study. Beautiful despite its immensity, it displays a largeness of kindly feeling not commonly surmised from Fairy tales of Giants and Giant deeds. The spectator gazes upon the grand old sleeper with feelings of admiration and awe. "Nothing like it has ever been seen," say all who have gazed upon it. "It is a great event in our lives to behold it," (is the universal verdict,)--" worth coming hundreds of miles for this alone." "I would not for anything have missed seeing it, for I consider it the greatest natural curiosity of the age," say Geologists, Naturalists, Students and all who can intelligently examine the Onondaga County Wonder.

The increasing interest of the public and the constantly enlarging attendance corroborate the previously expressed opinions of the inestimable value of the discovery, and sanction the verdict that the Cardiff Giant is the great wonder of the Nineteenth Century.

The American Goliah

The giant exhumed in 1869.
From a stereo photograph by Calvin O. Gott.

What Is It?

This question has been diligently asked and variously answered. Dr. John F. Boynton, of Syracuse, a celebrated Geologist, went among the first to the scene and examined the figure with much care. His opinion, (which was the first one expressed by any distinguished scientific authority) has been given decidedly that the body is a massive and beautiful statue. His own language will best state his reasons for declining to think it a petrifaction. A letter of his is subjoined, which was kindly furnished by him for publication. The letter was written to one of the most scientific men of America.

SYRACUSE, Oct. 18th, 1869.
Henry Morton, Prof.
in Pennsylvania University and Franklin Institute:

DEAR SIR:--On Saturday last, some laborers engaged in digging a well on the farm of W.C. Newell, near the village of Cardiff, about 13 miles south of this city, discovered, lying at about three feet below the surface of the earth, what they supposed to be the "petrified body" of a human being, of colossal size. Its length is ten feet and three inches, and the rest of the body is proportionately large. The excitement in this locality over the discovery is immense and unprecedented. Thousands have visited the locality within the last three days, and the general opinion seems to be that the discovery was the "petrified body" of a human being.

I spent most of yesterday and to-day, at the location of the so-called "FOSSIL MAN," and made a survey of the surroundings of the place where this wonderful curiosity was found. On a careful examination, I am convinced that it is not a fossil, but was cut from a piece of stratified sulphate of lime, (known as the Onondaga Gypsum.) If it were pulverized or ground, a farmer would call it plaster. It was quarried, probably, somewhere in this county, from our Gypsum beds. The layers are of different colors--dark and light. The statue was evidently designed to lie on its back, or partially so, and represents a dead person in a position he would naturally assume when dying. The body lies nearly upon the back, the right side a little lower; the head leaning a little to the right. The legs lie nearly one above the other; the feet partially crossed. The toe of the right foot, a little lower, showing plainly, that the statue was never designed to stand erect upon its feet. The left arm lies down by the left side of the body, the forearm and hand being partially covered by the body. The right hand rests a short distance below the umbilicus, the little finger spreading from the others, reaching to the pubes. The whole statue evidently represents the position that a body would naturally take at the departure of life.

There is perfect harmony in the different proportions of the different parts of the statue. The features are strictly Caucasian, having not the high bones of the Indian type, neither the outlines of the Negro race, and being entirely unlike any statuary yet discovered of Aztec or Indian origin. The chin is magnificent and generous; the eyebrow, or supercilliary ridge, is well arched; the mouth is pleasant; the brow and forehead are noble, and the "Adam's apple" has a full development. The external genital organs are large; but that which represents the integuments, would lead us the conclusion that the artist did not wish to represent the erectile tissues injected.

The statue, being colossal and massive, strikes the beholder with a feeling of awe. Some portions of the features would remind one of the bust of De Witt Clinton, and others of the Napoleonic type. My opinion is that this piece of statuary was made to represent some person of Caucasian origin, and designed by the artist to perpetuate the memory of a great mind and noble deeds. It would serve to impress inferior minds or races with the great and noble, and for this purpose only was sculptured of colossal dimensions. The block of gypsum is stratified, and a dark stratum passes just below the outer portion of the left eyebrow, appears again on the left breast, having been chiseled out between the eyebrow and chest, and makes its appearance again in a portion of the hip. Some portions of the strata are dissolved more than others by the action of the water, leaving a bolder outcropping along the descent of the breast toward the neck. The same may, less distinctly, be seen on the side of the face and head. I think that this piece of reclining statuary is not 300 years old, but is the work of the early Jesuit Fathers of this country, who are known to have frequented the Onondaga Valley from 220 to 250 years ago; that it would probably bear a date in history corresponding with the monumental stone which was found at Pompey Hill, in this county, and now deposited in the Academy at Albany. There are no marks of violence upon the work; had it been an image or idol of worship by the Indians, it could have been easily destroyed or mutilated with a slight blow by a small stone, and the toes and fingers could have been easily broken off. It lay in quicksand, which, in turn, rested upon compact clay.

My conclusion regarding the object of the deposit of the statue in this place, is as follows:--It was for the purpose of hiding and protecting it from an enemy who would have destroyed it, had it been discovered. It must have been carefully laid down, and as carefully covered with boughs and twigs of trees which prevented it from being discovered. Traces of this new decomposed vegetable covering can be seen on every side of the trench, and it is quite evident this vegetable matter originally extended across and above the statue.

Above this stratum of decayed matter, there is a deposit of very recent date, from eighteen inches to two feet in thickness, which may have been washed in, and likewise turned on by plowing. A farmer who had worked the land, told me that he had "back furrowed" around it, for the purpose of filling up the slough where the statue now lies.

The American Goliah

The Newell Farm, 1869.
The tent over the Giant is at the right.
[Onondaga Historical Association.]

It is positively absurd to consider this a "fossil man." It has none of the indications that would designate it as such, when examined by a practical chemist, geologist or naturalist. The underside is somewhat dissolved, and presents a very rough surface, and it is probable that all the back or lower portion, was never chiseled into form, and may have been designed to rest as a tablet. However, as the statue has not been raised, the correct appearance of the under surface has not been determined, save by feeling as I pressed my hand as far as I could reach under different portions of the body, while its lower half lay beneath the water.

This is one of the greatest curiosities of the early history of Onondaga county, and my great desire is that it should be preserved for the Onondaga Historical Society. Efforts are being made by some of our citizens to secure this in the county where it belongs, and not suffer it to bear the fate of other archeological specimens found in this region.

Hoping to be able to write you more in a few days,

I remain yours truly,
JOHN F. BOYNTON."

The American Goliah
Is The Body A Petrifaction?

"The majority of visitors disagree with the opinion of Dr. Boynton, that the figure is a statue, and pronounce it a petrified man. It is claimed that no sculptor would have invented such an unheard of position and design for a statue. No sculptor could have so perfectly imitated nature, especially in the minutiae which render the image such a wonder. It is claimed by the stone cutters and quarrymen who are constantly engaged in cutting the Onondaga County stone, that no single block could have been found of sufficient size, without a seam, from which to have chiseled out such a monster, (they claiming that the seam would have caused any such statue to split and fall apart under the necessary concussions required for cutting it to anything like its perfection in form.)

Other persons argue that no model of such a human being would have been likely to have been presented to any of the Indian or other inhabitants of America, within the past few centuries.

Many also ask for what reason should such an immense and expensive statue be hewn out and placed in so unfrequented a part of the country? How could it have been transported from the region of rocks to its present location, in a swamp entirely free from stones) especially since it is completely without any base or support of stone on which it can rest." "No statue is known to have been constructed," say the petrified advocates, "in reclining posture, unless the artist left some portion of the block of stone upon which the figure should rest, and be supported and strengthened for a durability of ages."

Other incidental suggestions are set forth as follows, by a writer in the Syracuse Daily Standard. "

The probabilities of its being a petrifaction have a better foundation, independent of outward appearances. First, is the fact that within a very short time, in the work of grading on section six of the Cazenovia & Canastota R.R., the skeletons of five mammoth human beings were exhumed, one of them eleven feet tall. The point of exhumation is not twenty miles distant from Cardiff. There are proofs of a giant race on this continent, and in this part of it; how far back, no one can tell. Second--There is now in the possession of the Onondaga Historical Association, a fish near one foot long, petrified to a perfect stone solidity, which was found near Cardiff, and the color of this petrified fish is very similar to the Cardiff giant stone. Mr. W.B. Kirk, of this city, when living at Cardiff many years ago, found near there a good sized Perch, that was perfectly petrified. Third--Five miles further down the valley, at what is known as the Onondaga Valley Cemetery, in taking up a human body for removal some years ago, it was found to be solid stone; still further north, but in the same range, the corpse of a child, on being taken up was found to be petrified--solid stone.--Still another case--the body of a man who had been buried a few years was taken up for removal, and being found a perfect petrifaction, the widow had it taken home, and it is yet retained in the house, and has never been reburied. We might give names, but do not feel at liberty to do so without first consulting family friends or relatives. These, and other samples that might be given, prove that petrification is not uncommon in the vicinity of Cardiff, where our ten feet two and a half inches, and well proportioned, giant was found."

A different statement still is made by Mr. Wright, father-in-law of Mr. Newell, who formerly owned Mr. Newell's present farm. Mr. Wright says that within a short distance of the present discovery, there is a spring of water which will within a few months turn into solid stone any small deposits of sand and gravel. Neighbors corroborate the statement. A wag has suggested that a factory be at once established there and petrified dogs, cats and small fry generally be furnished to order.

The unsettled point of what it is, undoubtedly furnishes an additional attraction regarding the mysterious stranger, as every person wishes to see for himself and become judge in the trial of Statue versus Fossil.

In this connection an interesting letter is subjoined from the Hon. George Geddes.

To the Editor of the Syracuse Standard:

--I find a notice in your paper of this morning of the "Stone Giant" at Cardiff, in which the fact that I visited it yesterday is stated, with the remark that you are told that I believe it to be a petrifaction. Allow me room in your paper to say that this is stating my views a little stronger than I desire. I have formed no opinion as to the origin

The American Goliah

of this wonderful thing. I was not allowed to make an examination of it beyond the privilege of looking from over a railing into the pit where the giant lay, and this pit was shaded by a tent, and the railing surrounded by double and triple rows of people, all anxious to see. I do not complain that I was not allowed a more perfect examination; there were too many to see to allow the descent into the pit of any one. All questions by me of the gentlemen in charge were politely answered. My impressions were decided that I saw before and below me the figure of a giant in stone of some kind, but what kind I could not tell for in that light and position it did not resemble any rock that our system has in it. I thought it was quite unlike our limestone or our gypsum formations; and that if it was sulphate of lime, and the work of human hands, that it was more likely to have been built up, than hewn from a solid rock. But as I have said, I had no means or liberty to make a close examination. I wish to say in addition, that I have traveled far and spent much money to see things of not one-tenth the interest that this stone giant was to me, and thought I had made good use of time and money.

Respectfully yours,
GEORGE GEDDES.
Oct. 20th, 1869.

The exhibition tent behind the barn on the Newell Farm.
[Onondaga Historical Association.]

What Is The Character Of The Surroundings Of The Image?

The spot is perhaps twenty-five feet below the house. The soil on the surface is a loose one, half sand and half muck (dark.) The spot has undoubtedly been filled in to a considerable extent from washings from the hills around. Mr. Wright, the former owner, says that the spot used to be covered with water, and that he had at one time a bridge constructed over this very point, in order to reach the higher land beyond. Even after the water failed to stand there constantly, he was obliged to use the bridge, as the soft muck was four or five feet deep, and was impassable for cattle and teams. The Onondaga Creek was within twenty rods of the spot, and at some seasons of the year overflows it. Some suppose the channel of the Creek was once there. The place had been a regular swamp for years. Mr. Newell has owned the farm for three years, and has occasionally ploughed around and thrown in dirt, to the depth of at least a foot.

Under the three or more feet of muck is found a strata of gravel from two to six and eight inches in depth. The body rests in and upon this gravel bed. The gravel under the neck of the image was very solidly pressed down. Underneath the gravel is found red clay, into which the gravel is pressed.

The right limb is perfect all around with slight exceptions. The left arm is perfect nearly to the hand, excepting that the shoulder is worn off some by the water underneath. The bottom of the right foot seems to be perfect. Some slight portions of the left foot have been cleaved off.

The family and the neighbors give, it might be remarked, an original hypothesis of their own, regarding the death of the man; viz: that in passing along over this spot he was either drowned or swallowed up in the mire and suffocated to death.

How To Find The Giant

Passengers by the Central or Oswego Railroads leave the cars at Syracuse, and will find an excellent road through the beautiful Onondaga Valley, to Mr. Newell's residence, twelve miles from Syracuse. Strangers will find the principal hack stand of the city near the Wieting Block, on Salina street. The entire force of drivers became within three days perfectly acquainted, not only with the road, but with the leading facts regarding the wonderful discovery. The demand for carriages has been immense, and is constantly increasing. If parties desire to spend the day at Cardiff, they can take the Syracuse & Binghamton Railroad to Lafayette Station, and (with considerable difficulty,) secure a team across to Mr. Newell's house, a distance of about three miles. There is no village at Lafayette Station.

Who Visits The Wonder?

Everybody. Old and young, male and female, people of all classes of community, rush in a constant stream to view the immense curiosity. People from all parts of the United States are hastening to see the Giant before he shall be removed from his long resting place. The average daily attendance for the first week was from three to five hundred persons.

The Cardiff Giant at the Farmers Museum, 1960s. From a postcard.

How Long Will He Be Kept?
Where He Was Found?

Probably for some time, as that seems to be the public wish. Arrangements have been made for some of the chief scientific men of the country to examine critically the colossus. Their opinion or opinions, (which will be published promptly in this work,) will have much weight in the minds of the managers in deciding when and what to do.

Who Owns The Image?

Three capitalists have bought of Mr. Newell, (who has declined probably over one hundred offers,) a three-fourths interest in the enterprise. The tour partners will determine what course to pursue.

We subjoin several reports of the Press for a few days succeeding the discovery of his Giantship.

From the Syracuse Daily Standard Oct. 18th, 1869.

The valley of Onondaga has a romance of beauty in its wild scenery, and as the home of the famous tribe of the red men of the forest-- the Onondagas--around whose council fires the chiefs and young warriors of the Six Nations assembled to consult on matters of great moment. It commences at the head of Onondaga Lake, having a broad surface where the main part of our city stands, and moderate hill-side boundaries, until we pass two miles south of the city bounds, where the bed of the basin begins to narrow away and the hills on either side to be more abrupt and higher. It continues to decrease in width, until it terminates against Tully Hill, a distance of fourteen miles from the lake. Its beauty of wild scenery is perhaps in greatest perfection in that part known as the Indian Reservation--still held by the Onondaga tribe--somewhat south of the centre of the valley. Two main roads lead up the valley, one at the base of the hills on either side; and riding along either of them in a pleasant day, an admirer of nature's wild grandeur has ample occasion of admiration. The gentle slope, rising way back and up as if touching the clouds, and the more abrupt and ragged, shrub-covered, not less high hills, miniature mountains, with every now and then a ravine down which the water leaps playfully along till it reaches the plateau below and into the little creek on its way to the ocean--is a landscape of beauty not easily described.

Just now this valley is the scene of an excitement, in the finding of a supposed petrifaction of a human being--a giant. The point of interest is on the south side of the valley, opposite and just beyond the little village of Cardiff, in the town of Lafayette-- twelve miles from this city, on a farm belonging to Mr. William C. Newell.

The American Goliah

On Saturday last Mr. Newell thought to dig a well some six or seven rods east of his house, and a trifle south-east of his barn. The spot is probably thirty feet below the house, and the surface soil is a loose, half sand, half dark muck, the natural washing from the hills above. It is not more than twenty rods from the creek, the channel of which is thought to have been at or very near this spot many years ago. Mr. Newell and a hired man, in digging, had gone down but two and a half feet when something hard was struck, which was believed to be a stone. They thought but little of it at first, expecting to have to break it loose and pry it out. But throwing out a few more shovels of earth from its side, the feet of a man appeared. A few minutes more of labor exposed the legs to the calf; and now their interest being excited, they began to dig carefully around it, until the whole form of a man--petrified giant--was brought to view. The neighbors began to hear of what was found, and of course went at once to see.

Mr. Silas Forbes, who resides a mile and a-half distant, came to the city Saturday evening and apprised us of the new found wonder, and Sunday we went to see it. The story was a big one, and not liking "Silver Lake Snaiks," we wanted to see before telling our readers. And here is what we saw:--

The form of a man lying on his back, head and shoulders naturally flat at hip a trifle over on right side; the right hand spread on the lower part of the abdomen, with fingers apart; the left arm half behind, and its hand against the back opposite the other; the left leg and foot thrown over the right, the feet and toes projecting at a natural angle. The figure was of apparent lime stone, a mixture of the gray and blue, common in most parts of the county, and seemed perfect in every particular. The muscles are well developed; the ribs might be counted; the nostrils are perforated so as to admit a large sized finger up near two inches; the lines of toe and finger nails are plainly marked; the left ear is partially gone, but the right one is perfect and in proportion to the other parts; the nose finely shaped; the forehead high; and the "Adams' apple'" at the throat just projecting out, is as most common with men. The appearance of the "countenance" marks the Giant of the Caucasian race, and not the Indian. If a work of art, the artist has failed in any effort at hair on the head.

The American Goliah

We have said that the whole was perfect. And so it appeared, except a few flakes dropped off while the work of exhumation was going on; and perhaps others yesterday. If any well proportioned man will make measurement of himself as above, he will see a striking agreement of ratio.

Though the figure has all the appearance of stone, nevertheless the outer surface shaves off with a knife without materially dulling the blade. This was tried, but of course was not allowed to proceed to disfigure Mr. Giant. A scale that fell from the bottom of one of the feet, looks much like gold quartz, but still is softish and crumbles readily, with a sort of soft sand stone result. It rests on half sand, half clay bottom, the earth above being, as we have already said, of a lighter character.

News of this remarkable discovery rapidly spread, and yesterday when we were there, people were coming and going, from a circuit of four or five miles around, in farm wagons, carriages and buggies, and on foot, to see it.

John A. Clarke, Esq., being at Cardiff, Saturday evening to speak on temperance, took occasion for a lamp-light view. Returning to the city near midnight, he told the story; and was telling it all day yesterday. Not one in fifty of his hearers would believe the counselor, generally esteemed reliable though he is. Still, before the day was over a dozen or more went out to satisfy their curiosity, and returned with full confirmation--and more too, and the "petrified Giant" is now the absorbing topic.

Mr. Newell has stumbled upon an "elephant" in this Giant. His neighbors say it is a fortune to him. It is averred that he was offered $5,000, $10,000 and even $20,000 for it; that a clergyman offered his farm in exchange for the monster--but these offers were all declined. We talked freely with Mr. N. He was quiet and modest, and we doubt if he has received any such proposals, except perhaps jokingly. He indicated no such thing. Yet he seemed anxious to have the "thing" brought out all right if possible, be it what it may, and therefore guards it by day and by night.

During Saturday night the surface water had settled in the pit so as to cover the image. The wise men of Cardiff were consulted. One said, bail out the water--exposure to the air will do no harm. The other said, leave it thus until some scientific man comes to decide as to the prospects of destructibility. And the latter's advice was adopted. Yet, when the water was undisturbed and clear, the whole could be seen perfectly plain. Later in the day Dr. J.F. Boynton, the geologist, drove out with Mr. John Geenway, the water was bailed out, and Dr. B. made a thorough inspection of his Giantship, put his arms under the neck, and fairly hugged the monster. The general impression is, that it is a petrifaction of one of those large human beings of which all of us have heard so much in our youthful days, and have read accounts of in maturer years--not here, but somewhere else. A book lies before us, having account of several, varying from eight to eleven feet; but we stop not to extract therefrom. Prof. Boynton, from a hasty examination, is of opinion that it is a work of art--a sculpture from stone. If this theory be correct, it would be scarcely less interesting than if a petrifaction. In the one case arises the speculation as to a gigantic race of beings that may have inhabited portions of this "new world" hundreds of years before Columbus discovered it; the other as to how long ago the artist did the work, and where came he, or his ancestors, from? Men nigh on to a hundred years, and who have resided in the county seventy of them, have never heard allusion to such a thing; the Indian traditions speak not of it. The record of the first white man in this region--Catholic Jesuits--is of something over two hundred years. That record preserves matters of less interest than this would be, but not this. Then again we say it would have scarcely less interest as a work of the chisel, than a petrifaction.

Our city is talking about the Giant. The story has passed from one to another till very many, probably ten thousand, of our citizens have already heard it. The interest is great in it, insomuch that it has been almost impossible for us to thus disjointedly write about the great wonder, because of the constant interruption by visitors who are anxious to hear from one who has actually seen.

From the Syracuse Courier, Oct 18th, 1869.

On Saturday morning last the quiet little village of Cardiff, which lies in the valley about twelve miles south of Syracuse, was thrown into an excitement without precedent, by the report that a human body had been exhumed in a petrified state, the colossal dimensions of which had never been the fortune of the inhabitants of the little village to behold, and the magnitude of which was positively beyond the comprehension or the understanding of the wise men of the valley. We are told that there were giants on the earth once; and, if the reports of those who have investigated this discovery are true, and that they are we have no doubt, this stony man--who for hundreds of years may have slept untouched and undisturbed, had it not been for the rude hand of a Cardiff farmer--must have been one of them. The excitement in and around Cardiff extended until it reached the City of Salt, and all day yesterday the discovery was the chief topic of conversation at the hotels and public places in the city. Of course, the most extravagant stories were told, and greedily devoured up by gaping listeners. Some would have it that the body exhumed was twenty-five feet high, and proportionately large. All day yesterday crowds visited the scene of the discovery, and returned to tell the tale of the wonderful discovery to their eager friends.

From the Standard, October 23d.

LETTER FROM REV. MR. CALTHROP.

DEAR SIR—

As everyone is deeply interested in the Onondaga Giant, perhaps it may be as well for each of us to add his mite towards guessing at the solution of the problem he has silently set us all.

It is no wonder that so many are of opinion that he is a gigantic petrifaction. His proportions are so perfect, and his appearance is so life like. I will add, that every one wants to think so. If he proved to be a petrifaction, what a realm of awe and mysterious conjecture would he open to us. But I, for one, feel convinced that he will prove to be statue, and for these reasons:--

First, I think there are evident marks of stratification in the stone. The left eyebrow and the top of the nose are the parts most elevated. These correspond exactly, both being composed of a white layer. On the chest is a squarish layer of a dark tinge; around, and slightly below this, is another layer corresponding exactly with the ins and outs of the first. Beyond, and below this, another and another all alike, seeming to be simply lines of stratification. The level seems exactly kept. Follow with your eye any two adjacent lines, and you will see that where they are close to each other the surface has an abrupt change of level; where they are further apart the surface is nearly horizontal. Where the surface approaches the perpendicular, as on the sides, the dark line showing the separation of the strata is thin, because it has been cut through nearly at right angles. Where the surface is more horizontal the dark line is broader, because it has been cut through obliquely, the breadth varying steadily with the angle of inclination. The same can be plainly seen along the right leg.

Another strong reason for its being a statue lies in the fact that not a single limb is detached. The right arm is not merely glued to the body throughout, as well as the hand, but it has the appearance of only being cut into the stone to a depth sufficient to give due relief. This is equally true of the left arm, and of the two legs, which are joined to each other throughout. The sculptor has not wasted a stroke of the chisel. I would add here, that between the third and fourth fingers of the right hand, the slit is carried too far toward the wrist, seemingly by a slip of the chisel.

Who did it? A trained sculptor; one who had seen, studied and probably reproduced many a work of art; one who was thoroughly acquainted with human anatomy. One, too, who had noble original powers; for none but such could have formed and wrought out the conception of that stately head, with its calm, grand smile, so full of mingled sweetness and strength.

He appears, however, to have worked under certain disadvantages. He had not such command of materials as a civilized country could have afforded him. He had to put up with the best stone he could find. I think that the peculiar posture of the statue can be fairly explained by supposing that the original block tapered away toward the feet, and was only just about the breadth of the statue as we now see it. This seems fairly to explain the curious position of the left arm. The artist had to put it there because there was not breadth enough to put it in any other position. So of the position of the feet--one over the other. The stone may not have been wide enough to have admitted of any other position. Who was he? Let us analyze a little.

In the ancient world, only the Greek School of Art was capable of such a perfect reproduction of the human form. I have seen no Egyptian or Assyrian sculpture which approached this in anatomical accuracy.

Throughout the middle ages till the great Art Revival, no one in Europe had skill enough for the purpose. It appears, therefore, that unless we adopt the somewhat strained hypothesis that a highly civilized society, now utterly extinct, once existed on this continent, we are forced to search for our sculptor among the European adventurers who have sought homes in North America during the last three centuries, as no one, I presume, is prepared to maintain a that the statue has a Greek or Roman origin, unless, indeed, it was brought over as an antique by some forgotten amateur of art.

Was it not then as Dr. Boynton suggests, some one from that French colony, which occupied Salina and Pompey Hill, and Lafayette? Some one with an artist's soul, sighing over the lost civilization of Europe, weary of swamp and forests, and fort, finding this block by the side of the stream solaced the weary days of exile with pouring out his thought upon the stone. The only other hypothesis remaining is that of a gross fraud. One need only say with regard to this that such a fraud would require the genius of a sculptor joined to the skill and audacity of a Jack Sheppard.

But lastly, what did he intend it to represent? Had he known of the discovery of America by the northmen, he might have had in his thoughts some gigantic Brown, or Erio, or Harold. The old northman is shot through with an Indian's poisoned arrow; his body is dying, as the tight pressed limbs express; but the strong soul still rules the face, which smiles grandly in death. If you had objected that there was too much mind shining through the features, the sculptor might have answered that the closed eyes saw in prophetic vision that men of his race would one day rule where he had lain down to die. But this is rather too high flown, so I had better conclude.

Yours,
S.R. CALTHROP.

The American Goliah

Transporting the Giant to Syracuse.
Engraving from Harper's Weekly, Dec. 4, 1969.

Letter Favoring Petrifaction.

MR. EDITOR:--

It needs no apology to address you upon a subject that is now engaging the constant attention of all your readers and thousands besides, and if any person can throw any light upon the subject it would seem to be their duty to communicate it to the public. While there has been much speculation and wonder as to the nature and origin of the marvelous curiosity found last Saturday in the town of Lafayette, in this county, there has been made public no argument from scientific men up to this time to settle the doubts and convictions of the unlearned. In the suggestions which I shall make upon the subject, I regret that I have not the benefit of a more extended knowledge of the sciences which pertain to the subject, but having earnest convictions, supported apparently by plausible reasons, I submit them to the consideration of the public for whatever weight they may be entitled to.

The advocates of the theory that the subject in question is a statue, have too many difficulties to overcome to establish their position.

If the subject is a statue it must have been formed by some person, who once lived, and had an object or motive for making it. Who can say what that object was? It must have been formed by a

The American Goliah

person of wonderful genius and skill. Where and when did such a person exist? History gives no account of him. Its formation and object must have been known to many persons who assisted in its manufacturing and transportation. Where are those persons?

The objections to the theory that the figure in question is a statue, may be briefly described as follows:

1st. This figure, if made by human hand, was intended to be exhibited; otherwise there can be no motive for making it. If it was intended to be exhibited, it was also designed to assume some position, either an erect or recumbent one. The reasons for keeping it in that position would have been provided by the sculptor, by either making a pedestal for it to stand upon, a tablet for it to lie on, or forming the body on the stone out of which it was cut, so that it would lie upon a flat surface. Nothing of this kind is visible. There is nothing about the figure remaining except what belongs to a man who has lain down alone in solitude and agony to die and has died, and the story of whose death has been preserved by the miraculous agencies of nature.

Second, if designed by man as the representation of man, the head would have been covered with hair, the most beautiful ornament of the human body, yet no trace of hair is found on this subject.

Third, it has been claimed that the material of this figure is gypsum taken from the hills of Onondaga county. The evidence of our most experienced quarrymen is that a block of gypsum of sufficient size to make this figure was never found in this region.

Fourth, if this figure was sculptured from marble or stone, its body, head and limbs would be solid. Yet the orifices in its wasted rectum and other parts of its body, and the resounding noise occasioned by striking upon it proves that it is hollow internally.

Fifth, No statue was ever sculptured in this or a similar position. The position is precisely that which a person would assume who was suffering an agony which was to result in death. The hands pressing opposite sides of the lower part of the body and one leg drawn up and pressed against the other is the effort of expiring humanity to relieve itself from pain. The sculptor's chisel and the painter's brush have often been called upon to represent scenes of death in all its various forms and manifestations. Yet have they never attained the simplicity, the impressiveness, the vivid naturalness of the story told by the figure which lies in yonder clay.

Sixth, It should also be observed that a sculptor who had the genius to form such a figure would naturally keep a proper and harmonious proportion in the different parts of the body, but it will be noticed in this subject that the feet are unusually broad, projecting far beyond the natural lines of the leg, and giving evidence of usage which has caused what is almost a deformity.

Seventh, If a statue, why should one of the eyes differ so much from the other, one of them being open, and one nearly or quite shut?

Eighth, If this figure is a statue, explain how it has been transported and handled to place it in its present position. It is estimated by the best judges that the figure weighs from a ton and a half to two tons. This immense weight could not have been transported by any known means of transportation in the neighborhood of the figure, and it could not have been handled without the aid of machinery.

Ninth, Perhaps the greatest objection to the statue theory is the last on which I shall mention, and that is the majestic simplicity and grandeur of the figure itself. It is not unsafe to affirm that ninety-nine out of every hundred persons who have seen this would have become immediately and instantly impressed with the idea that they were in the presence of an object not made by mortal hand, and that the figure before them once lived and had its being like those who stood around it. This feeling arises from the awful naturalness of the figure and its position. No piece of sculpture of which we have any account ever produced the awe inspired by this blackened form lying among the common and every-day surroundings of a country farm yard.

We see objects of larger size every day, formed from materials which excite our wonder or admiration, and upon which have been bestowed the highest skill of the artist, the sculptor and the painter, but there is in that blackened mass, that worn and impaired as it is by the action of the elements, and repulsive from the nature and color of the material forming it, which inspires an awe and reverence such as the handiwork of a mortal, no matter how gifted, has ever accomplished. I venture to affirm that no living sculptor can be produced who will say this figure was conceived and executed by any human hand. But Mr. Editor I am afraid I have trespassed too far on your attention and space. There is much more to be said on the subject, which at a future time I will say.

R.

The present owners of the Giant have engaged Col. J.W. Wood, known all over the country as a popular showman, as their manager. To-night Mr. W. will have a much larger tent (forty feet) over his giantship, so that hereafter many more can be accommodated at a time--whether they can see better we are not sure.

From the Syracuse Journal, October 23d, 1869.

SPEAKING OF THE CARDIFF GIANT.

Reports of Committees. Three of us--Tom, Dick and Harry--interviewed the stone wonder on Thursday of this week, and here are our reports. Tom sees everything from a ludicrous point of view, and is nothing if not funny. Dick is a common-sense fellow, who makes up in positiveness what he lacks in education; and I am—

Yours, very respectfully,
A.C.

TOM'S REPORT.

His Majestic Highness was in bed when we reached the royal residence although it was high noon by the dial.

But the obliging janitor was convinced, by a single glance at the cards we presented, that it would not do to refuse us admission. We found the Noble Duke divested of wearing apparel and enjoying his morning ablution, which was administered by a valet de chambre, who stood on a platform above His Excellency, and held him down with a ten foot pole. The countenance of the great man expressed composure and serenity. His eyes were closed and his general appearance and attitude were limp and cadaverous, causing us to fear, for a moment, that His Mightiness might be dead instead of sleeping.

The American Goliah

Our apprehensions were allayed, however, when the irreverent attendant punched his Sublime Majesty in the head and chest, and elicited an impatient, cavernous, responsive "ugh!"

Having feasted our eyes on the unveiled grandeur of the stupendous Knight, we begged permission of his keeper to get into the Imperial bed and embrace the gigantic feet. We begged in vain. Let us then grasp that autocratic right hand, which reminds us so touchingly of the dear, fat, fried-cake hands Bridget used to mould for us in our infancy. Our request was declined with emphasis. May we not breathe an affectionate word into that dexter ear, which seems placed far down towards his shoulder as if on purpose to receive our tender message? "He's deaf," said the heartless man with the pole. Let us at least give him one-- just one--kiss for his mother. "He never had no mother," responded the inexorable valet, and we turned sadly away from the Kingly presence of the sweet, sleeping orphan.

As we wended our homeward way we gave ourself up to meditation, while our companions gave themselves up to sandwiches and boiled eggs.

We called to mind the striking resemblance in form and features, which the vast monarch bears to the Stoneman family, and we rejoiced that a gallant General of our army could trace his ancestry to one who stood so high in the community.

From appearances we should judge the seraphic Emperor to be a man of property--worth at least fifty thousand dollars.

Whether he were so or not, we certainly were petrified-- with astonishment.

Yours for the right,
THOMAS.

DICK'S REPORT.

There's no use talking; that fellow was once a living and breathing human being. In my opinion he walked these hills and valleys, just the same as we do, thousands and thousands of years ago. We read of the sons of Anak, but this chap was the father of Anak. It is beyond the art of man to carve so perfect a human being out of stone. Anybody who could sculp like that could have made his fortune, without hiding his work away and letting it be discovered by accident in after ages. And who ever saw a piece of statuary in such a position, and without hair on?

The man that says that this petrified man is nothing but a graven image, proves that he is a little soft in the upper story. There is no shadow of doubt that this is a genuine petrifaction. I would take my oath of it. Dr. Boynton writes a long rigmarole to show that he is a statue made by the Jesuits; but in my opinion the Dr. is just laying low so that he can buy the curiosity and make his pile on him. Why, you can see the very cords in his legs, where the flesh has decayed off; and the matter running out of his right eye has turned to stone. Would the Jesuits have been likely to carve cords and tears? The idea is too absurd to be thought of. This is my report, and I don't care what anybody else says.

RICHARD.

HARRY'S REPORT.

Whether the colossal figure be a petrifaction or a piece of statuary, it is a mystery and a success. Who carved it?. When was it made? Whom does it represent? What is its lesson? Why was it hidden? How happens it that tradition is silent about it? These are puzzling questions, which at present are solved only by conjecture.

Let no one imagine that he has an adequate conception of this wonder till he has seen it, with his own eyes. Description seems to be no aid whatever; ocular inspection is positively necessary.

He who fails to see the curiosity in its present locality and position, will have reason to regret this neglect or misfortune all his life time.

I was not permitted to make a careful and thorough examination.

"Hands off," was the imperative order of the proprietor, and I bowed to the decreer. I craved permission to apply a drop of acid in order to determine certainly whether the material was gypsum or ordinary limestone, but my request was denied. If on the application of acid there had been no effervescence, the inference would be that the specimen was not limestone, the material of which petrifactions are usually composed. But although chemical tests and manipulations were prohibited, there seemed to be no disposition to forbid the use of our eyes--at a respectful distance. And the proprietor very kindly refrained from exacting a promise that we would not express an opinion, if we should have temerity enough to form one.

I take it that this specimen was carefully placed in its present locality. Had it been washed from a distance, it would have been fractured and mutilated, and it would not in all likelihood, have lodged in its present easy and natural position.

If this were once a living man, he must have died ages and ages ago. If buried, the accumulated deposits upon his grave, in this low piece of ground, during thousands of years would have been deeper than three feet. If he were drowned, or if he lay down on the surface of the earth to die, the flesh would have decayed and dropped from his bones without petrification. If he were petrified in his present locality, we ought to find other petrifications in its immediate neighborhood, whereas all the twigs and branches which covered and surrounded him are free from the slightest encrustation.

Human bodies do not petrify in layers; but the strata in the Cardiff giant, especially on the left side, are as manifest as they are in a ledge of rocks. The eye brows, the tip of the nose, the breast and the thigh are of the same stratum, and the layers in the right arm are clearly of different degrees of density.

The conclusion seems irresistible that the giant is a work of art rather than of nature. The sculpture must have been done some years ago, or the lower parts of the figure would not have crumbled and been washed away by the sluggish oozing of the water through the soil.

Its age cannot antedate the present race of men, for the shape of the head and the features are entirely modern. The old-time people, as portrayed in the sculpture of Assyria and Egypt, had no such heads as this. The artist evidently took a corpse for a model and proportioned his colossal figure by careful measurement. He was thus enabled to secure the general anatomical accuracy for which his giant is remarkable. He followed the model very closely, not attempting to represent a living being, not venturing even to supply the missing hair. And these omissions, the result of inexperience, furnish, singularly enough, the principal arguments to the petrifactionists. For the popular opinion that the body and head are hollow, that the nostrils and other orifices are open, and that the tendons in the decayed leg are visible, has not the slightest foundation. Why was this image made? Why hidden? and by whom? are questions which I must be excused from answering at present.

HENRY

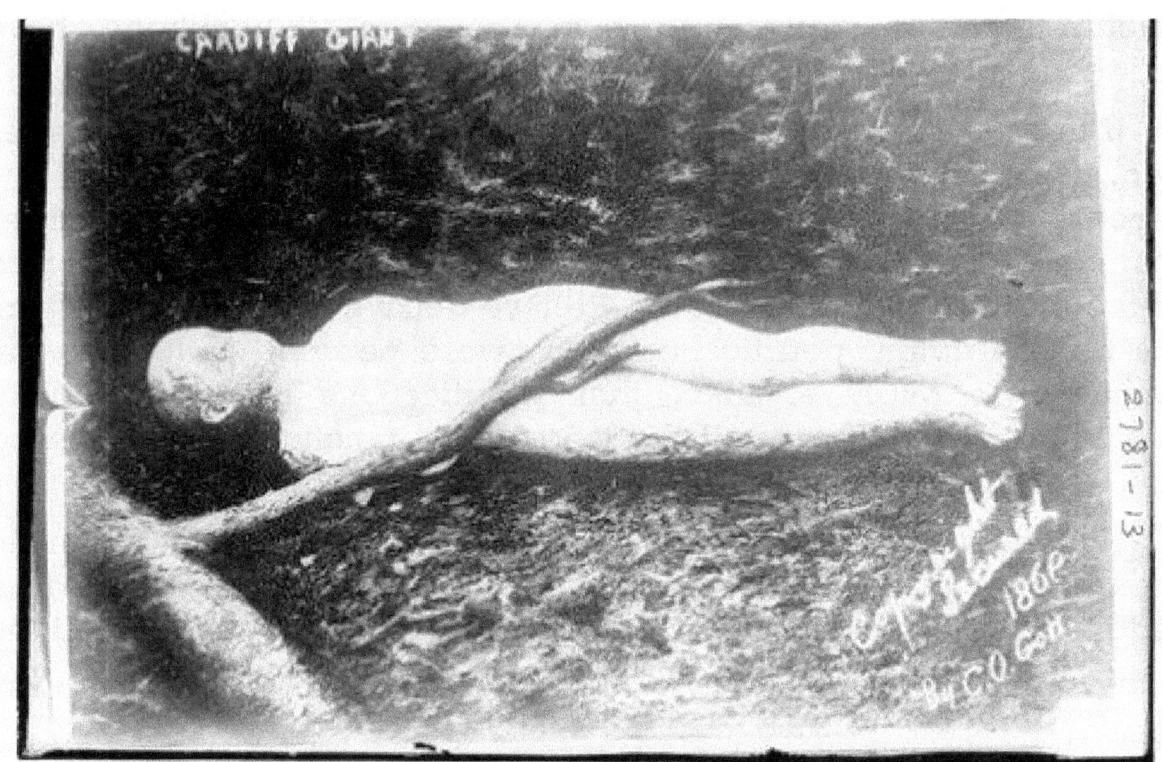

The Belief Of The Onondaga Indians
The Body Of An Indian Prophet.

To the Editor of the Syracuse Journal:--

In your columns devoted to "Letters from the People," I thought you would at this time publish the following, it being interesting as one of the current opinions of the Indians of "the Castle" regarding the wonderful "human petrified statue," which, in its colossal proportions and the sphynx-like silence of its history is so electrifying and exciting the people.

By one of the old squaws I am told that a large number of Onondagas believe that the statue is the petrified body of a gigantic

The American Goliah

Indian prophet, who flourished many centuries ago, and who foretold the coming of the pale-faces, though long before the foot of our forefathers had touched the western continent. He warned his people with prophetic fervor of the coming encroachments of the white man, and the necessity of their abstinence from a poison drink he would bring to craze and destroy them. He told them that he should die and be buried out of their sight, but that THEIR DESCENDANT WOULD SEE HIM--AGAIN.

J.P. FOSTER,
State Agent and Teacher
for the Onondaga Indians.

The Stone Giant.

On Saturday the sale of the remaining one-half interest in the Great Giant Wonder was closed up. Another partner, Mr. Wm. Spencer --an old-time schoolmate of Mr. Newell--was taken in, so that the present owners are Wm. C. Newell, of Cardiff, Alfred Higgins, Dr. Amos Westcott and Amos Gillett, of this city, David H. Hannurn, of Homer, and Wm. Spencer, of Utica.

Saturday was a bad day, as to weather; nevertheless several hundred visited the Giant.

Sunday was a crusher. The people began to go early, and kept going all day long. From eleven to three o'clock it was a dense mass of people on the Newell farm. Around the house and barns acres were covered with teams and wagons, and the road, for a long distance in either direction, was lined with them. It seemed as if such another jam never went to a show before, and it was with great difficulty that the line could be kept so that all could have a fair sight. All the proprietors were on hand, and did all they could to accommodate the crowd. At three P.M. twenty-three hundred tickets had been sold, Mr. Higgins bringing in the $1,150 received therefor, for safety. Not less than three hundred tickets were sold after three o'clock, so the total number of visitors for the day would be 2,600.

The Tully story of fraud is exploded. The mysterious man said to have visited that village, etc., turns out to be no other than a cousin of Mr. Newell's, a resident of Binghamton, and a tobacconist. He was on the grounds all day yesterday, and frankly told all there was of his visit at the time alleged, to the satisfaction of every one.

Letter From A Petrifactionist.

EDITOR STANDARD:--

Permit me to notice a few of the arguments upon the Cardiff discovery, appearing in your paper of Saturday last, and the Journal of the same day.

It seems a committee of the editors and owners of the Journal, named respectively Tom, Dick and Harry, of widely various characteristics, visited the Giant last week, and treat the subject on their return by articles published in that highly original sheet, according to their respective peculiarities. Tom, who is evidently admired in his family circle as a man of great humor, has so cultivated that faculty that it presents an abnormal development, and if petrification ever does overtake him, posterity may hope it will not operate upon his intellectual faculties. Dick, on the other hand, is gloomily satirical, and by the aid of that useful faculty utterly annihilates his opponents without saying anything. But last, Harry takes up the theme and treats it in a spirit becoming the gravity of the subject.

He thinks that the artist formed the figure according to a pattern, having a cold "corpse" conveniently by as a model, from which he could take "careful measurement," and proceeded to make this figure, not attempting, he says, to make this corpse look like a "living figure," which certainly was modest in the artist. He also says that he did not attempt to "supply the missing hair." The question very naturally arises here, "Why was the hair missing, and how long had the corpse been a corpse to lose its hair? and was it a pleasant occupation to do business with such a corpse?" This omission (i.e. to put on hair), Harry says, arose from "inexperience."

Now, experience is certainly an excellent thing, and when properly acquired and wisely used is undoubtedly of considerable benefit to mankind. But that it was necessary, in order to enable an artist to know that hair grows on the human head, we had not before supposed. Into such absurdities, oh Harry, does he run who abandons his familiar scissors for the unaccustomed pen.

The American Goliah

I will briefly refer to the letter of Rev. S.R. Calthrop in favor of the statue theory. While it shows the scholarship of its author, his thorough appreciation of artistic influences, and the wonderful imitation of nature produced by the one who formed this figure, it does not seem to me to go very far towards proving his position. Starting off with the idea that many reasons may be given against the theory of petrification, he commences with number one, and then he stops; it is true he gives one other reason, but neglects to number it; and the two reasons are--

First, that evidences of stratification appear on the body, thereby assuming that they would not appear in a petrified body; and, secondly, that the separate members of the body are not detached from each other as they were in life, assuming also that this does occur in cases of petrifaction.

Are these assumptions correct as matters of fact?

The evidence as to the existence of strata in this body is very conflicting. A number of professional persons who visited this figure on Saturday, and subjected it to close scrutiny with a powerful magnifying glass, and who all, by the way, hold the "statue theory," say there were no evidences of stratification in the body; that what appears to be such is simply the difference in shading, produced by the greater or less density of the material composing the figure. The appearances indicating stratification are also explainable by the action of the water, charged with carbonate of lime, upon the body. The line of contact between the body and the water would necessarily receive a deposit of lime, causing a straight line of lighter color to appeal oi the body. It is also a fact, which I have learned from quite a number who first visited the body when it was submerged in water, that the present water level leaves exposed the nose, eyebrow and breast at the points where some persons now think they see stratification. In fact, deposits of carbonate of lime of a whitish color, even now, adhere to the left ear and side of the face which show the presence of that substance in the water, and that it will adhere to and become a part of the subject with which it is brought in contact.

Now, how is stratification produced in the formation of stone and rocks. It is said by geologists to be formed only when the original material forming the rock or stone has been transported and deposited by the operation of a body of water holding the material in solution, and depositing it in alternate layers at its place of destination.

How is a petrified body formed? Science answers, that it is formed by the gradual infiltration of silicious earth, pyrites of iron, carbonate or sulphate of lime, into the pores of the body, taking the place of the decaying parts, and substituting a new and original substance to take the place and form of the body petrified. These substances are always conveyed to their place of destination, and then applied to accomplish their purpose by the operation of water. The petrified substance may have none of the material composing the original figure, and the nature of the body formed either assimilates to the material around it, or is determined by that of which it is composed. So also all of the substances forming petrifaction may be found together in the same subject, or they may accomplish their work separately.

Silicious earth goes largely to form flint quartz and the various kinds of sandstone carbonate of lime, of limestone, and so of the other materials mentioned forming their peculiar kinds of stone. I have heard one statue-theorist trying to prove that the decayed portion of one of the legs showed the presence of flint, and therefore he argued it could not be a petrifaction. Not so. It probably would prove, if true, that the figure was not a statue, for pieces of flint are not found in such material, unless it be a petrifaction, in which case silicious earth would account for it. Now it is safe to say that there is no substance that enters into the composition of stone that does not enter into the formation of a petrifaction.

Now, these materials are, in cases of petrifaction, brought to the spot and deposited by action of the water--precisely such an operation as forms strata of rock; should it not produce the same effect in the appearance of successive layers or strata in the subject of petrifaction? With reference to the other objection to the theory of petrifaction, viz:--that the members of the body are conjoined and not detached--it is sufficient to say, from the very nature of the operation of petrifaction, portions of the body lying in contact would necessarily be conjoined and filled up. The wasting portions of the body are silently but surely supplied by nature, and as the transformation progresses, nature causes her deposit to adhere to its proximate kindred matter, and forms thus a solid and adhering body.

It is also somewhat worthy of observation that fossiliferous remains occur more frequently, than elsewhere, in marshy and swampy places in this country. Thus the low marshes known as the "Blue Licks" in Kentucky, and other similar places abound in specimens of fossil remains. These are often, indeed, quite commonly found near the surface of the ground, and it is a fact that the material and formation of marshy grounds change less through the operation of time than other places. The Pantine Marshes and the Marshfield Fens have preserved forms and characteristics for centuries upon centuries. Why is it then, that we are to be driven for a solution of the question as to the character of this curiosity to a hundred improbable and unnatural suppositions, when the thing may be explained by perfectly natural causes without violating any probabilities?

It is somewhat amusing to talk with the various advocates of the "statue theory," as each successive one is sure to knock over his predecessor's structure before he begins to build his own.

The endless suppositions which are produced to account for this marvelous work as a production of the sculptor are certainly a great credit to the imaginative faculties or inventive genius of our people, but people of ordinary intelligence find it hard to believe that men of wonderful genius and skill inhabited our original forests for the purpose of producing gems of art and then burying them in the marshes, or that men of culture and education go traveling in a wild and barbarous country encumbered by a piece of statuary weighing about two tons and being necessarily somewhat inconvenient to carry in our pockets.

Yours,
Com.

Opinion Of Professor Hall, State Geologist.

Professor Hall, gives the following definite opinion, in the Albany Argus of Monday, the 20th of October:

The American Goliah

GENTLEMEN:--

Your paragraph in this morning's issue, relative to the Onondagas Stone Giant, does injustice to the proprietor of that most remarkable object.

Dr. Woolworth and Prof. Hall left here on Thursday afternoon, with the intent of visiting, as they had been solicited to do, the supposed fossil giant or statue--for there were conflicting opinions in regard to its nature. On Friday morning they left Syracuse for Cardiff with Dr. Wieting and Judge Woolworth of the former place. As soon as practicable after their arrival, the tent was cleared of visitors, the party named were admitted and left to their undisturbed investigations for a full quarter of an hour; and when it is understood that the crowd outside were enough to twice fill the tent, and all desirous of seeing, and that the receipts of the owner for tickets were $26 per hour, it seemed scarcely civil to occupy a longer time.

The Giant, as has already been stated, is a statue of crystalline gypsum (not a cast) lying upon its back, or slightly inclining to the right side, and in an attitude of rest or sleep. The head is directed to the east, southeast, and the body, without support or pedestal, lies upon a thin stratum of gravel, which has been covered by about three feet or more of fine silt, in the bottom of which are some partially decayed roots or branches of trees-- doubtless floated there at the beginning of the silt deposit. The water, oozing from the southwest, along this gravel bed, has dissolved that side of the statue and gives it a pitted appearance, such as masses of gypsum or limestone acquire when long exposed to the action of the water. The earth at the sides of the pit bear no evidence of having been disturbed since its original deposition, and, to all appearances, this statue lay upon the gravel when the deposition of the fine silt or soil began, and upon the surface of which the forests have grown for succeeding generations

Altogether, it is the most remarkable object yet brought to light in this country, id altogether, perhaps, not dating back to the stone age, is, nevertheless, deserving of the attention of archaeologists.

H. Albany, NY,
October 23, 1869.

The American Goliah

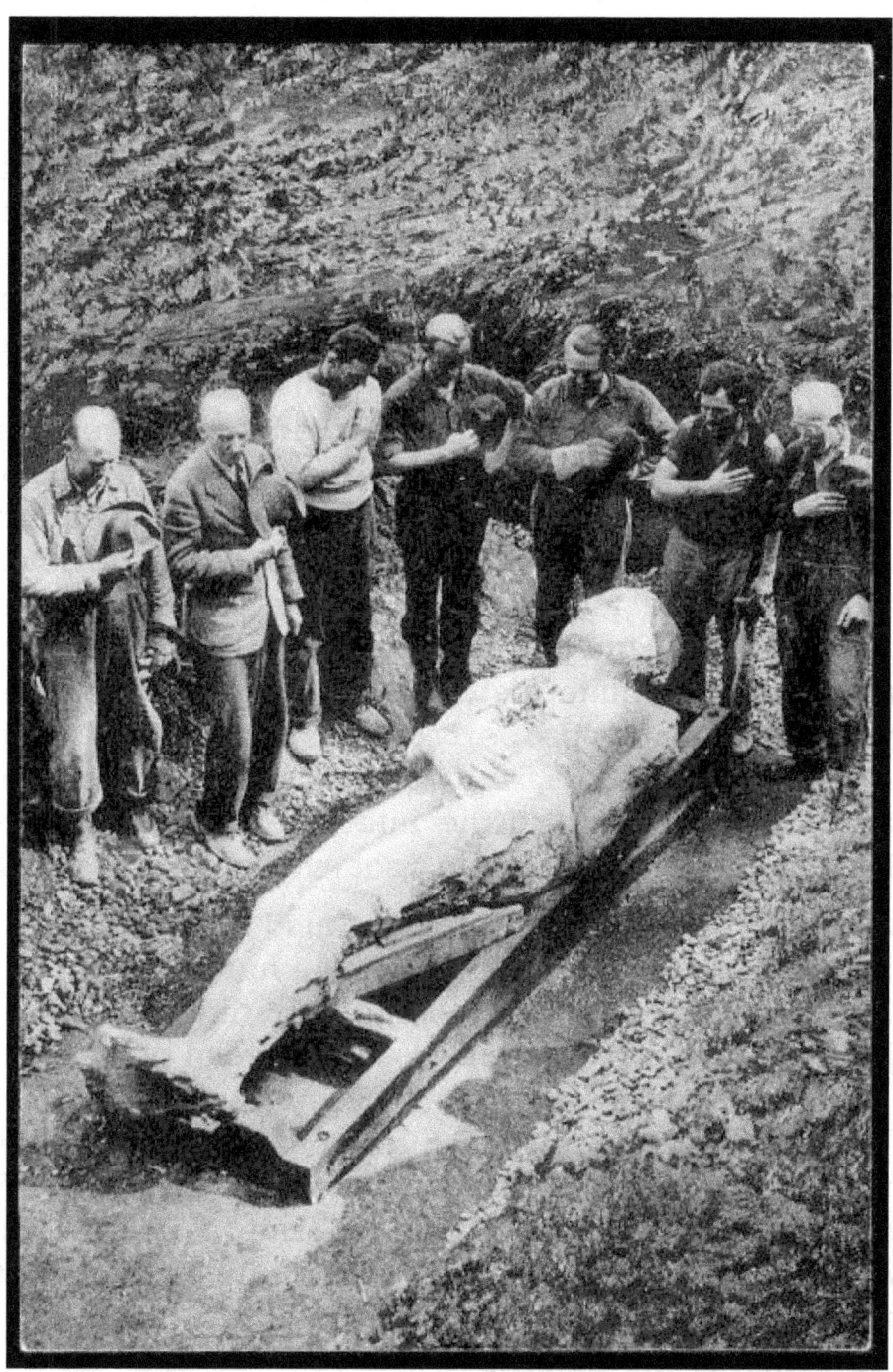

The American Goliah

From the Syracuse Journal Oct. 25, 1869.

More Than A Nine Days' Wonder.

The Onondaga Giant proves to be much more than a nine days' wonder. --Sunday completed the nine days of excitement and marvelings over this remarkable discovery, and instead of an abatement of the popular interest, it would seem that it has but just begun to be awakened. The attendance of visitors on Sunday was largely in excess of that of any previous day, and the number reached nearly three thousand. A new and large tent had been (erected, with increased accommodations, but it was found wholly inadequate to accomodate the crowds that occupied it from early morning till late in the evening. The agent for the proprietors raised a British flag over the tent, explaining that he thought some flag ought to be displayed, and that this was the only one he had there --a circumstance that was quite distasteful to very many of the visitors. An American flag has now properly been substituted. The number of visitors to-day is quite large, and as the people of the surrounding country are just waking up to the interest of the exhibition, many thousands will yet go to see it in the spot where it was unearthed.

The interest in the subject abroad is also now fairly developing. The discovery was at first looked upon as a humbug, but this view is giving way before the facts presented in the local papers. The leading journals of the country have sent special correspondents to write up the subject. The New York Tribune and Herald, Harper's Weekly, the Springfield Republican and other papers, have already had their representatives at the scene of the discovery. The new proprietors, --who are now stated to be Messrs. William C. Newell, of Cardiff, Alfred Higgins, Dr. Amos Westcott and Amos Gillett, of this city, David H. Hannum, of Homer, and William Spencer, of Utica, propose to continue the exhibition where it has thus far been held, till difficulty in reaching the locality occurs from bad weather, then to remove the giant to this city, where it will remain till the local curiosity is satisfied, and then convey it to New York and other leading cities for public exhibition.

The American Goliah
The Value Of The Giant Wonder.

We learn from a reliable source that $20,000 was offered on Saturday by a perfectly responsible party and in good faith, to two different persons holding interests in the stone giant, for one-quarter share of the stock in the wonderful statue, and the offer was promptly declined.

An Ancient Coin Found In The Earth Taken From The Giant's Bed.

On Saturday last, Mathew, a son of Dr. Alexander Henderson, veterinary surgeon, of this city, while visiting the Cardiff giant, picked up from the surrounding debris thrown out of the excavated resting place of this huge work of stone something that seemed like a blackened scale of brass or a rusty old button. Thinking that it might have some affinity to the wonderful statue, the lad rubbed the dirt and rust from its surface between his finger and thumb, and burnishing it a little by rubbing it in the folds of his coat skirts, it showed evidence of being an old copper coin, and he accordingly placed it carefully in is pocket, and brought it home. Dr. Henderson, the lad's father, applied some acids to it, when an ancient coin, of nearly the eleventh century, revealed itself.

On the obverse side of the coin is the head of the Emperor Jestyn, with a full flowing beard from the chin, and the sacred heart strung from a rosary in the shape of a shield, or breast-plate, strung around the neck. Beneath the Emperor is the date, "1091," and around the edge of the coin is the following inscription-"JESTYN-AP-GURGAN, TYWYSOG--MORGANWG." The interpretation of this, as rendered by a competent Welshman, means, "Jestyn, son of Gurgan, Prince of Glanmorgan." On the reverse side is the figure of the Goddess of Commerce, seated on the wheel at her side, the pillar and ancient crown, wreathed with the national emblem, the oak, the shield and spear supported by the left hand, and the right hand pointing to a ship on the distant sea, with full sails set, which she seems intently gazing at. The inscription around the circle is in the Welch language, and reads as follows:--"Y. BRENAIN-AR- GYFRAITH," the interpretation of which is "The King and the Laws." The coin is 778 years old--over seven and a half centuries--and on the edge of the rim can be distinctly seen "Glenmorgan Half Penny," with representations of leaves intertwining. The denomination of the coin is imprinted in raised letters, and everything connected with it shows it to be a coin of the reign of the emperor whose name it bears. Further, in connection with the unearthing of the stone giant, its discovery in the loose dirt thrown up from the bed of the excavation where the statue was found, and yet lies, is certainly quite interesting, and seems to add to the general interest that attaches to this great and unexplained mystery of the Nineteenth Century.

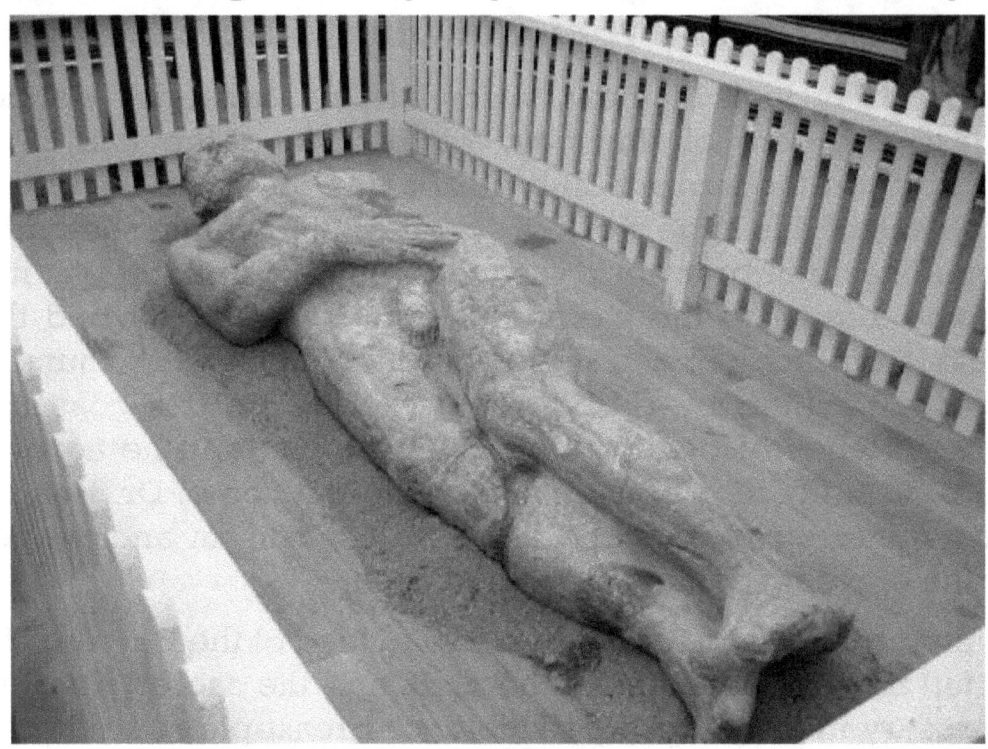

Probabilities That It Was Transported On The Water-Courses From The Sea-Board.

Although there are still intelligent advocates of the petrifaction theory, the preponderating weight of opinion supports the view that the giant wonder is a work of art. We understand all the scientific gentlemen, who have been permitted to make thorough examination, to be agreed in this decision.

The next question is, How did it come to be where it was discovered? There is very little probability that it was carved on the spot where it was recently exhumed; the stone for that purpose was not likely to have been found there or to have been taken there; and the situation where it was discovered, a morass or water-bed, favors the theory that it was deposited there. Setting aside the belief, honestly entertained by many people in the immediate vicinity, that the statue was surreptitiously placed in the slough where it was dug up a few days since, there is tenable ground for the theory that it was taken there by some of the early white visitors to this section of country. This might have been done by transportation over the water-courses communicating with the locality, either through the River St. Lawrence, Lake Ontario, the Oswego River, Onondaga Lake and Onondaga Creek, or through the Hudson and Mohawk Rivers, Oneida Lake and River, Onondaga Lake and Onondaga Creek. These waters were early navigated, and within the memory of persons still living the principal means of transportation was by batteaux, which with considerable loads were propelled along these water-courses. The Onondaga Creek was in those days navigable for light-draft craft capable of conveying a much greater weight than this statue, at least as far up its waters as the place of this discovery.

The place of the discovery is not in the original channel of the creek, but in a detour from that channel. It is not unreasonable to suppose that for some reason--from alarm, or from a desire to secret the object,--the craft was run out of the main channel into this then open water-way, where the statue was deposited.

The early Jesuit visitors to this vicinity may have had this statue in their keeping. It may have been fashioned by some of their number. It is not impossible, that it may have been brought here, or even have been carved out at some place not far distant, by other of the early visitors to this region. We expect that light will be thrown upon these speculations, by the scientific investigations, which will determine the exact nature of the material of which the statue is composed, by which alone some hint of its place of origin may be derived. The intimations given us by Professor Hall, in our brief interview with him, impressed us that he looked upon the statue as of great antiquity, antedating the present geologic period, and equaling in interest and importance the discoveries made in Mexico of archaeological remains, indicating a high degree of civilization in the tenth, eleventh and twelfth centuries.

When Was The Statue Put Where It Was Found?

The American Goliah

To the Editor of the Syracuse Journal:--

If it would not be asking too much, I would beg leave to say a few words through the columns of your paper. In Saturday's issue of the Standard I notice a letter written by "Skeptic," which that paper calls "silly," and charges the writer with being "lacking in the upper story." This is a misfortune, truly; but I have taken some trouble to investigate these reports and find them vouched for by highly respectable parties. There are, to my mind, several reasons for the belief that this wonder has not occupied its present position longer than is intimated in the above mentioned letter.

The soil where it was found is soft, and an excavation large enough to admit the object could easily be made in an hour or two. The location is favorable for such purpose, being behind the buildings, and hidden by the abrupt bank; a little straw or other litter would cover all traces. Then, if the stone man be moulded from cement, it would not weigh near what it would if cut from stone, and could be handled with ease by three or four men. This idea that the curiosity was cast or moulded, is strengthened by the fact that it has no other support than the ground upon which it rests. Had it been the work of a sculptor it would have had a tablet for support. Now, you ask, perhaps, where was the pattern made, if moulded, and how could the parties making the cast escape detection? I would ask, who carved it, if a stone, and where did the sculptor bring out such a work without the knowledge of the fact being discovered?

It is said by those who ought to know something about our gypsum quarries, that there are no such slabs of stone found there out of which this object could be carved. Further, it is allowed by all who have examined this wonder, that the head appears to have been hollow. Now, if the head is hollow, it is either a moulding or else it must be what those interested claim for it: a veritable petrifaction. No sculptor would carve the head in that condition.

But I have used too much of your valuable time, so I will close.

TULLY, Oct. 23d, 1869.
CONE WILLIAMS

Of What School Of Art Is This Statue?

To the Editor of the Syracuse Journal:--

The American Goliah

In the discussions relating to the "Giant," I find there are many who favor the Grecian and Roman school of sculpture. The Greeks and Romans excelled the early Egyptians in one thing only, that is representing the human hair. Their male statues have flowing and bushy locks and a beard. On the Egyptian statue, the hair looks more like a skull cap on the back of the head, than hair, with no indication of beard. They had been so afflicted with plagues through the Israelites, that they would have nothing that was like them, or that reminded them of them. The Cardiff giant has no beard and nothing on the forehead to indicate hair; behind the ears running up to the crown, there seems to be something, that when he is raised, may show the Egyptian school of sculpture. As art goes from one country to another, the style changes somewhat to suit the taste of the people. In America, at first, our sculptors and painters copied from the French and Italian schools, but put on a little more drapery, as our people were modest and would not bear a true copy. Time, the destroyer of all things, has turned the drapery into dust, and we now have the original in all its glory and shame.

W.

P.S.--A hard-shell brother at my elbow says he will go his bottom dollar that the Cardiff chap is the original "Poor Uncle Ned, who had no hair on the top of his head;" he has lain down there and got Klu-Kluxed. (Klu-Kluxed is a Greek word, and means petrified or dried up.) The only objection to his theory is, Uncle Ned's shin bone curved backward, this man's curves forward.

The American Goliah

The American Goliah
Cut Of The Giant.

We herewith present a wood cut of the Giant. We have waited for an engraving from a photograph, in order to insure in every part of the pamphlet the utmost accuracy. The taking the photographs having been delayed, we present a sketch until their completion. The owners of the Giant furnish this publication alone with photographic copies--which will appear promptly on completion.

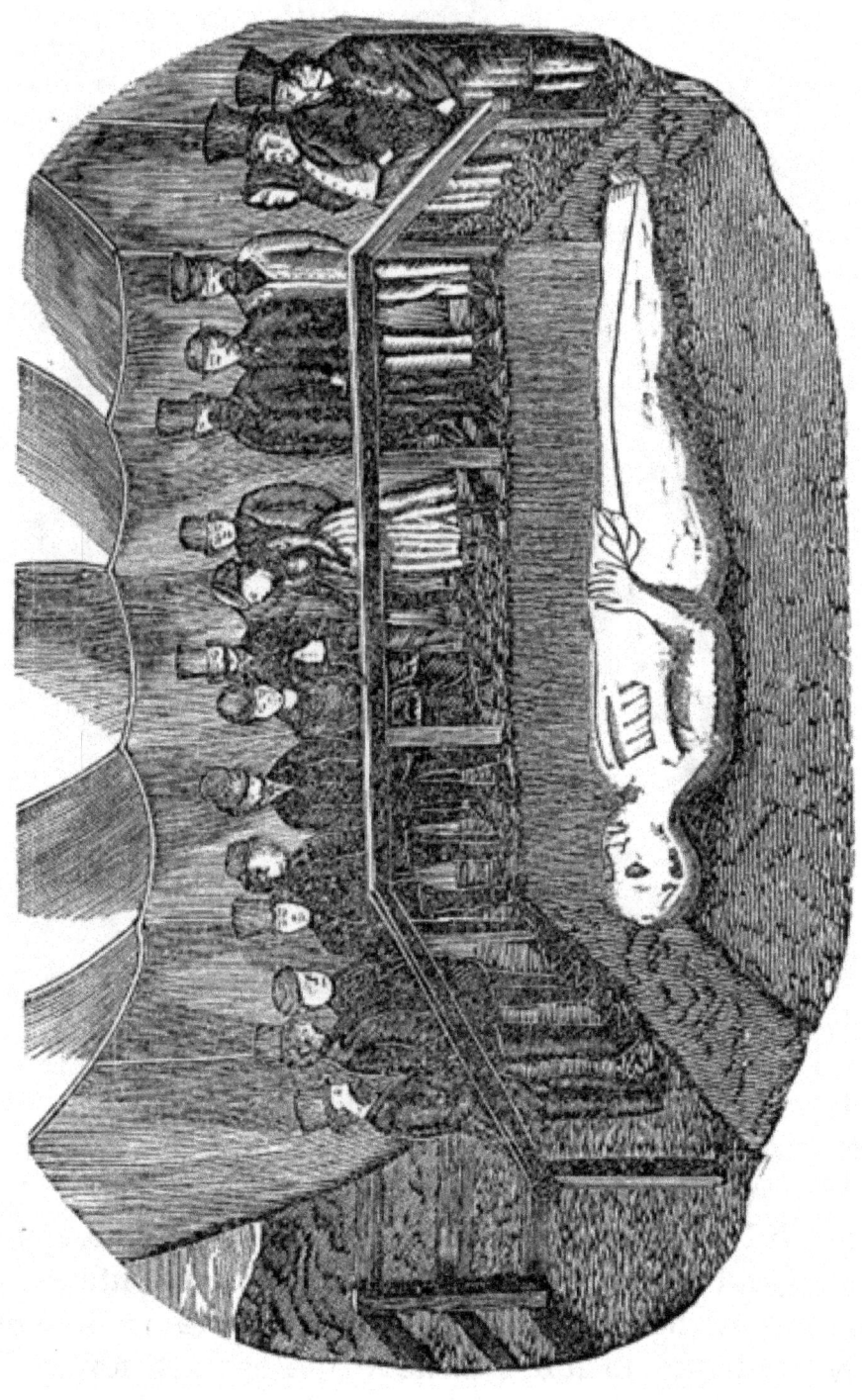

A Mite In The Scale.

To the Editor of the Syracuse Journal:-- Clark's "History of Onondaga," Vol. 1, page 43, near the bottom, says:--"The Quis-quis, or great hog, was another monster which gave the Onondagas great trouble, as did also the great bear, the horned water-serpent, the stone giants, and many other equally fabulous inventions, bordering so closely upon the truly marvelous, that the truth would suffer wrongfully if related in full; but nevertheless are found among the wild and unseemly traditions of the race."

H.

The American Goliah

Letter From Prof. Ward.

The following letter from Prof. Henry A. Ward appears in the Rochester Democrat, and will be found to be well worthy of perusal. Prof. Ward takes high rank among the scientific men of the country, and an opinion from him is certainly entitled to respectful consideration:--

EDITOR DEMOCRAT—

I have just returned from a hasty visit to the colossal statue, or "Fossil Giant," as many have called it, which is now causing so great an excitement in our sister city, Syracuse, and in all the country for many score of miles around.

This great archeological wonder is located in the Onondaga Valley, on the west side, about three-quarters of a mile from the village of Cardiff. The valley itself is one of erosion, dating its birth to the time when the gradual rise of our continent from beneath the ocean's waves had subjected all this portion of our State to the fierce furrowing and deep denuding action of violent currents of water, aided in their work by floating masses of ice and by rock debris carried by and often frozen into these masses. For about twelve miles south from Syracuse the valley is quite narrow, but here the hills recede on either side and sweep widely around in two high crescent-like ranges to meet again (or nearly so) at a point three or four miles higher up the stream. Within the sort of amphitheater thus formed, and at the foot of the western hill, is the farm of Mr. Newell. His house and outbuildings lie at the edge of the slope, and touching a low meadow which extends for a hundred yards or more to the bushy margin of a creek beyond. A smaller stream or a branch of this same appears at one time to have run close to the hill, leaving faint traces of its contour on the meadow, and one small elliptical swale or soft, boggy spot, a few yards across, near the lower corner of Mr. Newell's barn. It was while digging a shallow pit in this swale that the relic was found. It is a gigantic human figure lying on its back, with its head to the east and feet to the west. The head is in the position commonly given to a corpse; the right arm extends downwards, with the hand and fingers spread stiffly across the abdomen; the left arm bends down along the left side, with the hand quite under the middle line of the body; the left hip is raised a trifle, the thigh and leg more so, so as to bring the lower part of the left leg and foot obliquely across and over the same parts on the right. The posture is in all one that a dying body left to itself might naturally assume. The entire length of the figure is ten feet two and a half inches, and the other parts of the body are proportionately colossal.

Its head is of a very elongated type, but well shaped, and with a countenance full of solemn, dignified composure. The features are purely Caucasian, having neither the high cheek bones of the Indian, nor any other facial outlines which mark the type of other Aztec aborigines.

To describe the appearance of this great figure as being strange and impressive is saying too little.

Lying as it still does, in its original earthy bed, its grey massive form hardly yet still from the struggles by which it seems to have freed itself, and the face, body and limbs still damp with the ooze of its low sepulchre, it possesses the beholder with a feeling of extremest awe and profoundest wonder. To interrupt these emotions by speculations as to its personality, to approach this majestic figure with the calm processes of scrutinizing investigation, seems a sacrilege. All one's feelings persuade to accept it as a real human being, once instinct with life and activity, now a noble corpse. The proprietors of the giant figure, or statue, as we shall now call it, use all due effort to strengthen this feeling, and enlarge the belief that their wonderful discovery is really a petrified human being--a genuine" Fossil Man" preserved entire, with flesh and bones changed to stone in the very place where he fell at death, or possibly was buried by his coevals of an olden time. All opportunities of close examination are refused; indeed, the present throng of visitors would make such general permission impracticable. The little, darkened tent, and the pit shaded by a triple row of spectators, whose heads almost touch across it in their earnest efforts to see the body below, made it quite impossible for me to obtain that thorough acquaintance with the huge object which I would have liked. But I saw enough in the fifteen minutes (only) which are allowed to each set of visitors within the tent to fully satisfy myself of the true nature of the figure.

The American Goliah

The "Onondaga Giant" is the work of the sculptor, and out of a single large block of the gypseous limestone (an upper member of the "Onondaga Salt Group") which forms large beds in the immediate vicinity. This stone is very strongly marked by lines of deposition, causing bands of different shades extending in horizontal layers, perfectly even and parallel through large quarry masses. In the present in stance these layers are so disposed--in the way the sculptor chose his block--as to cut lengthwise through the whole body, and to mark off different leads over the entire figure. Thus the left hip and left breast present (cameo-like) a layer different and higher than the one which forms the corresponding parts on the right side of the body. The head, too, with its different elevation of chin, nose and forehead, is very strongly marked in the same way. These linings are well-known peculiarities in the original deposition of a stratified rock, and are not features assumed in the petrifaction of any organic body. Further peculiarities of the Onondaga gypsum are very noticeable in the block, and among them is the peculiar style of decomposition by which the whole lower part of the figure is affected, as also one side of its head. Here the soluble earths, with any portions of carbonate of lime, have been dissolved away, and the pure granular sulphate (snowy gypsum) remains, standing up with ragged, uneven, cavernous surfaces, which is a feature very noticeable everywhere in weather-worn fragments of this rock. This decomposition or rotting of the lower side of the left leg gives a very vivid semblance to the corruption of actual flesh, and has doubtless had much to do with the ready reception which the "petrifaction" theory has found among the mass of visitors--even including many men of intelligence and general education. If such persons will refer to works which treat of petrifaction in all their various kinds of transformation and in all the thousand genera and species of fossil organisms, they will find that although bones, shells, and the hard parts of animals, changed to stone, yet preserving their original outlines, are of constant occurrence, yet there is not a single instance on record of fossil flesh; of the fat, muscle or sinew of man or beast changed into stone or into any substance resembling stone. To a person acquainted with the nature of petrifaction, the slow substitution of mineral for animal matter, particle by particle, the reason why humor of other flesh does not undergo the same change will be apparent. This is truly not entirely in accordance with popular belief, nor with the ever-recurring stories in our public journals. "A fish nearly a foot long, petrified to solid stone" has lately been cited in your columns as another instance of the petrifactions of the Onondaga Valley. I visited this yesterday at the Museum of the Onondaga Historical Society, at Syracuse, and found (what I had before surely surmised,) a simple, short, club-like fragment of limestone, worn by running water to a form like a little fish. "This it was and nothing more."

It is proposed--and very properly--that this Onondaga relic should be submitted to the examination of Professor Hall, Agassiz, Leidz, or some other of our geologists known to fame and infallible

The American Goliah

experts in these matters. This were well. But there is another court which I think, would pass quite as prompt a decision. I believe that a sculptor, in examining this most singular specimen, would at once recognize its artificial character. The devices for saving time or for adding strength, partially cutting out the figure, are sufficiently apparent in the object before us. The legs--with their heavy thigh, the swollen knee portion, the swollen calf and slender ankle, all touch on the outline length as they lie over each other, with no open space between, or no point where one folds down upon the other with a sharp line of contact of the two surfaces. The same thing, too, is noticeable in the arms and in the fingers of the hand, where the flesh, instead of sloping away-- one rounded surface finely leaving another--is cut down square, as if some unnatural out growth of flesh had formed a uniting portion beneath the member. This is a too common device in the coarser grades of sculpture to escape notice here. Our sculptor would certainly find fault with the very constrained position of the body, its feet awkwardly crossed and its left arm twisted rather than laid backward under its body, certainly this is not the attitude in which a sculptor--a man of taste--would place his handiwork. Still, may it not be an admissible theory, that the old-time artist was constrained in the form which he should give his statue, by the form and dimensions of his gypsum block. If there was not material sufficient to carve out both arms lying across the breast, he might find enough to make one of the arms below. If the lower left hand corner of the block were broken off, he might still bring out both feet by lapping one over the other, and letting vertical space atone for lateral want of it. If our sculptor, finally, will look sharply upon the legs and body in such parts as have escaped the considerable water-wearing which has smoothed most of the figure, I think that he will see plainly the marks of the graving tool of his ancient colleague. But, as he now has the figure in charge--I positively rejecting it as being no fossil--I will leave to him and the Archeologist to study and puzzle upon it. Dr. J.F. Boynton, of Syracuse, (to whom, by the way, belongs the credit of having first discerned and recorded in print that this is a statue), says, "I think that this piece of reclining statuary is not 300 years old, but is the work of the early Jesuit Fathers in this country, who are known to have frequented the Onondaga valley from 220 to 250 years ago; that it would probably bear a date in history corresponding with the monumental stone which was found at Pompey Hill in this county, and now deposited in the Academy at Albany. All these are points which Archaeologists and Ethnologists may yet determine. Will not Hon. Lewis H. Morgan leave Rochester by an early Monday train and see this most wonderful statue while it is still undisturbed in its bed.

H. A. WARD.
ROCHESTER, October 23, 1869.

Letter From Gen. E. W. Leavenworth.

To the editor of the Syracuse Journal:--

This subject does not seem, even yet, to be exhausted, much as has been written in regard to it. Having spent an hour yesterday in the inspection of the great mystery, permit me hastily to give you the results of my observations.

THE LOCALITY.

For the benefit of the large number who will not be able to visit the locality, it may be well to define more fully and precisely the exact spot in which it was found. It is near the west line of the town of Lafayette, in the upper section of the valley of the Onondaga Creek, called Christian Hollow--a short two miles above the south line of the Reservation of the Onondaga Indians. The valley at this point is about half a mile in width, and there are two north and south roads running through it, directly at the foot of the hills on each side. The small village of Cardiff nestles under the eastern hills, about half a mile directly east of the locality in question, which is precisely at that point where the slope of the western hills meets the alluvial valley of the Onondaga Creek. This point is about one hundred feet east of the west road, and about two hundred feet west from the bank of the creek. On the west the ground rises moderately to the road, then more rapidly to the top of the western hills, some eight hundred feet above the valley below. On the east it is nearly or quite a dead level to the creek, the ground being evidently all alluvial. The valley is beautiful-- thickly settled and under high cultivation.

THE POSITION.

The American Goliah

The statue--for such I am sure it is--lies in a hole about twelve feet long, five feet wide at the top, and four at the bottom. The soil of the first three feet, or a trifle more or less, is the common alluvial soil of the Onondaga valley. The next foot is gravel, which rests on the solid clay. The ends of many pieces of wood project through the gravel and some are found in the soil above.

IS THERE ANY FRAUD OR DECEPTION.

Those familiar with the frauds practised in other countries in the manufacture and sale of antiques, and perhaps others, would have a vague suspicion that this might furnish another instance, nearer home. My own mind was not free from such dreams. And notwithstanding the apparent impossibility of finding a place where such a stone might be obtained--of quarrying, working, transporting, and burying the same, and keeping it a profound secret, I still had my suspicions. But the first look at the statue dispels from the mind every thought of that nature. It has the marks of the ages stamped upon every limb and feature, in a manner and with a distinctness which no art can imitate. I have not seen the first person who entertained any doubt of its great antiquity, after looking at that most wonderful and inexplicable figure. The time spent in manufacturing and retailing the simple and absurd rumors which circulate through the community and find their way into the papers, is weakly and foolishly thrown away. It is a serious and most remarkable reality, and one which as yet have received no satisfactory explanation, and probably never will.

IS IT A STATUE OR A PETRIFACTION?

Serious doubts are really entertained on this subject, and it is elaborately discussed. I must confess that I have none whatever, and for the following reasons:

First--There is no satisfactory evidence that any one person ever lived in any age or country of this world, of the statue of ten feet, unless it be Goliah of Gath. I know very well what is claimed and said on this subject, but the evidence would not satisfy a jury of intelligent men.

The American Goliah

Second--There is nothing in the general aspect, which leads any one to think it anything but stone. I venture to say, that were it in any other form, such a supposition would never have arisen.

Third--The stratification of the stone is perfectly visible, even to the imperfect observation now allowed. Mr. Calthrop's letter is full and satisfactory on this subject, but in addition to the places pointed out by him, the stratification may be seen on the left shoulder, and I think on the top of the head. That upon the left breast is, however, most clear, distinct and satisfactory.

Fourth--The whole statue, in all its parts, furnishes the most conclusive evidence, that it was all cut from one stone. It is quite clear that the stone has been cut away just far enough and only just far enough to show the legs, the arms and the fingers.

Fifth--The fracture of the stone along the left leg,, and especially on the heel of the left foot, which seems to be recent and fresh, is the fracture of our common gypsum, and leaves no doubt, so far as the eye can determine, that the material is stone.

It is said that on striking the head or the chest, it gives forth a sound indicating that the statue is hollow. Such evidence must in any event be very uncertain, and now no such experiments are permitted.

No one is permitted to touch the statue, but I was allowed to look at it with a powerful glass at my leisure.

I have carefully read the nine points made in the Standard of the 23d, to its being a statue. None of them are conclusive, nor, as it seems to be very strong, do they affect my belief on the subject. The marvelous has a great attraction for all of us, but we cannot afford to surrender our better judgment for the luxury of enjoying a belief in it.

In the meantime, why will not Mr. Newell run a dozen or twenty trenches from the locality of the giant, in every direction, down through the alluvial soil to the clay, and see if other discoveries may not be made, which will throw light on this one?

Very respectfully,
E.W. LEAVENWORTH,
SYRACUSE Oct. 20th, 1869.

From the Syracuse Journal, Oct. 27th.

Letter From Professor Hall, The State Geologist

ALBANY, Oct. 26th, 1869.

Messrs. Truair & Smith, Publishers of the Syracuse Journal:

GENTLEMEN:--

I have just received your favor of the 25th instant, in relation to the "Stone Wonder," visited by us. There can be but one opinion about it, I think.

It is a statue, cut in gypsum, and intended to represent a human form of colossal size in a recumbent posture. As to its source or origin, I cannot conjecture. It is worn and dissolved by water to a degree that indicates long inhumation, and it is covered by an alluvial deposit of three feet or more in depth. The sculpture is of a high order and very different from those of Central America. I enclose you a few paragraphs[1] which I wrote in reference to a statement that I had not been permitted to examine the object in question. I do not see that we can say more at present.

I am respectfully, your ob't servant,
JAMES HALL.

---

[1] The same letter communicated to the Albany Argus of October 25th, under the signature "H." and printed on page--.

The American Goliah

To The Giant of Onondaga.

Speak out, O Giant! stiff, and stark, and grim,
Open thy lips of stone, thy story tell;
And by the wondering crowd who pay thee court
In thy cold bed, and gaze with curious eyes
On thy prone form so huge, and still so human,
Let now again be heard, that voice which once
Through all old Onondaga's hills and vales
Proclaimed thy lineage from a Giant race,
And claimed as subjects, all who trembling hear
Art thou a son of old Polyphemus,
Or brother to the Sphinx, now turned to stone—
The mystery and riddle of the world?
Did human passions stir within thy breast
And move thy heart with human sympathies?
Was life to thee, made up of joy and hope,
Of love and hate, of suffering and pain,
In fair proportions to thy Giant form?
Did ever wife, by whatsoever name
Or tie of union, with her ministries
Of love, caress and cheer thy way through life?
Were children in thy home, to climb thy knee
And pluck thy beard, secure, and dare thy power
Or, was thy nature as its substance now,
Like stone--as cold and unimpressible?
Over these hills, with spear like weaver's beam,
Dids't thou pursue the chase and track thy foe,
Holding all fear and danger in contempt?
And, did at last, some fair Delliah
Of thy race, hold thee in gentle dalliance,
And with thy head upon her lap at rest,
Wer't shorn of strength, and told too late, alas,
"Thine enemies be upon thee?"
Tell us the story of thy life, and whether
Of woman born--substance and spirit
In mysterious union wed--or fashioned
By hand of man from stone, we bow in awe,
And hail thee, GIANT OF ONONDAGA!

SYRACUSE,
Oct. 20, 1869. D.P.P

The American Goliah

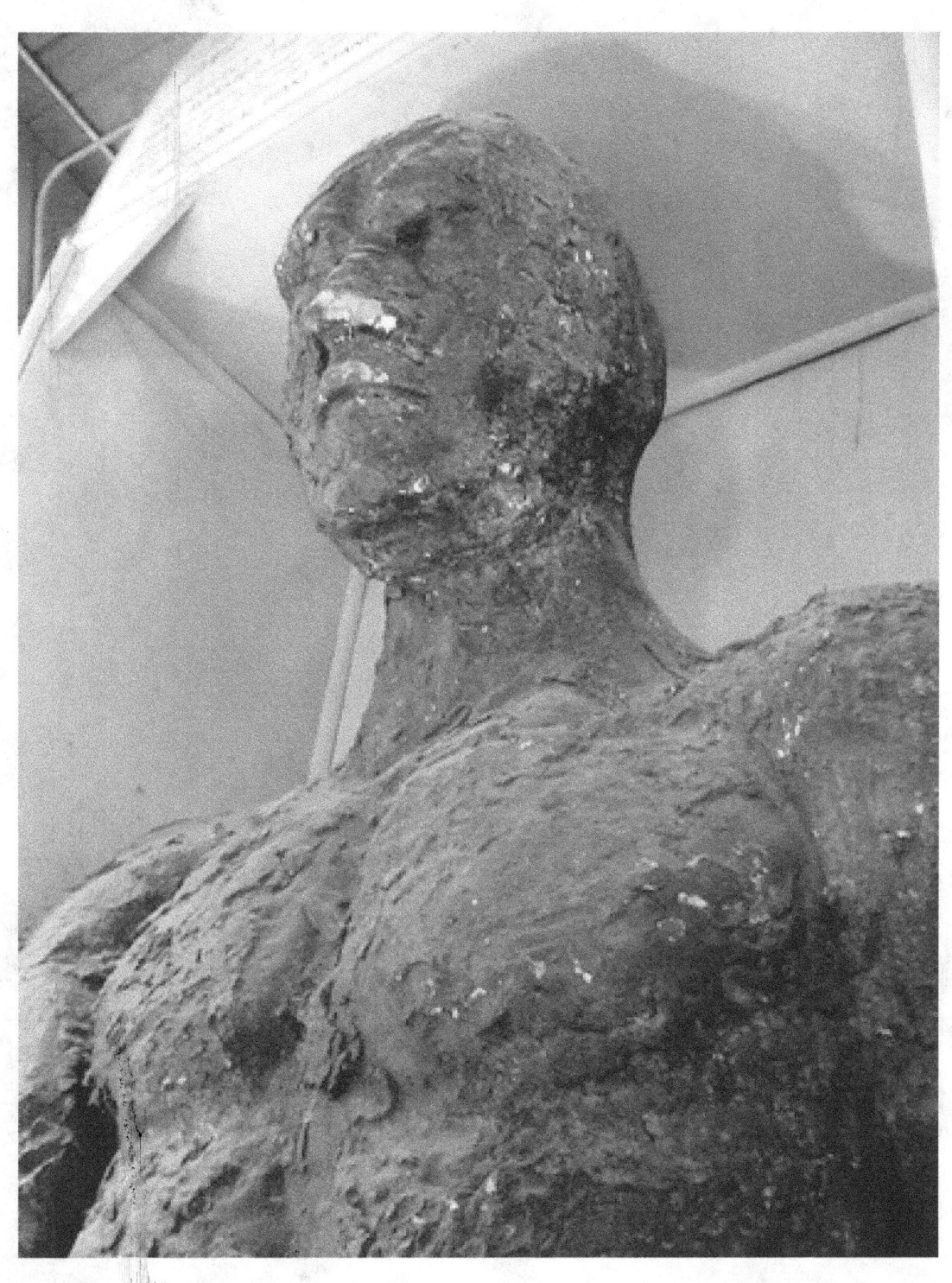

The American Goliah

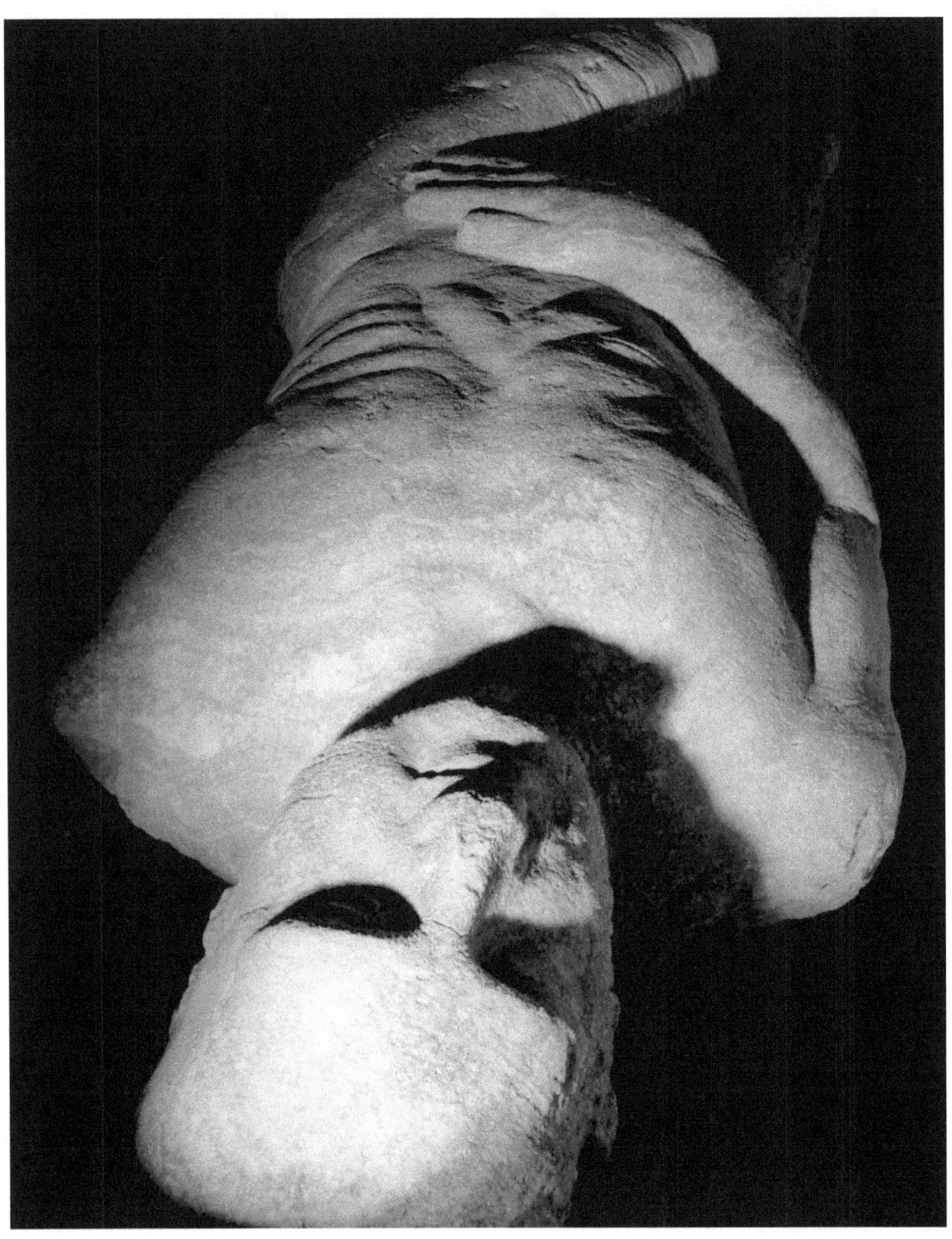

The Cardiff Giant:
A Chapter In The History
Of Human Folly
1869-1870
by
Andrew Dickson White
(1917)

THE traveler from New York to Niagara by the northern route is generally disappointed in the second half of his journey. During the earlier hours of the day, moving rapidly up the valleys, first of the Hudson and next of the Mohawk, he passes through a succession of landscapes striking or pleasing, and of places interesting from their relations to the French and Revolutionary wars. But, arriving at the middle point of his journey,—the head waters of the Mohawk,—a disenchantment begins. Thenceforward he passes through a country tame, monotonous, and with cities and villages as uninteresting in their appearance as in their names; the latter being taken, apparently without rhyme or reason, from the classical dictionary or the school geography.

And yet, during all that second half of his excursion, he is passing almost within musket-shot of one of the most beautiful regions of the Northern States,—the lake country of central and western New York.

Andrew Dickson White (1832-1918), diplomat, author and educator. Co-founder of Cornell University.

It is made up of a succession of valleys running from south to north, and lying generally side by side, each with a beauty of its own. Some, like the Oneida and the Genesee, are broad expanses under thorough cultivation; others, like the Cayuga and Seneca, show sheets of water long and wide, their shores sometimes indented with glens and gorges, and sometimes rising with pleasant slopes to the wooded hills; in others still, as the Cazenovia, Skaneateles, Owasco, Keuka, and Canandaigua, smaller lakes are set, like gems, among vineyards and groves; and in others shimmering streams go winding through corn-fields and orchards fringed by the forest. Of this last sort is the Onondaga valley. It lies just at the center of the State, and, although it has at its northern entrance the most thriving city between New York and Buffalo, it preserves a remarkable character of peaceful beauty.

It is also interesting historically. Here was the seat–the "long house"–of the Onondagas, the central tribe of the Iroquois; here, from time immemorial, were held the councils which decided on a warlike or peaceful policy for their great confederation; hither, in the seventeenth century, came the Jesuits, and among them some who stand high on the roll of martyrs; hither, toward the end of the eighteenth century, came Chateaubriand who has given in his memoirs his melancholy musings on the shores of Onondaga Lake, and his conversation with the chief sachem of the Onondaga tribe; hither, in the early years of this century, came the companion of Alexis, de Tocqueville, Gustave de Beaumont, who has given in his letters the thoughts aroused within him in this region, made sacred to him by the sorrows of refugees from the French Revolution.

It is a land of peace. The remnant of the Indians live quietly upon their reservation, Christians and pagans uniting harmoniously, on broad-church principles, in the celebration of Christmas and in the sacrifice of the white dog to the Great Spirit.

The surrounding farmers devote themselves in peace to their vocation. A noted academy, which has sent out many of their children to take high places in their own and other States, stands in the heart of the valley, and little red school-houses are suitably scattered. Clinging to the hills on either side are hamlets like Onondaga, Pompey, and Otisco, which in summer remind one of the villages upon the lesser slopes of the Apennines. It would be hard to find a more typical American population of the best sort–the sort which made Thomas Jefferson believe in democracy. It is largely of New

The American Goliah

England ancestry, with a free admixture of the better sort of more recent immigrants. It was my good fortune, during several years, to know many of these dwellers in the valley, and perhaps I am prejudiced in their favor by the fact that in my early days they listened very leniently to my political and literary addresses, and twice sent me to the Senate of the State with a large majority.

But truth, even more than friendship, compels this tribute to their merits. Good influences have long been at work among them: in the little cemetery near the valley church is the grave of one of their early pastors,–a quiet scholar,–the Rev. Caleb Alexander, who edited the first edition of the Greek Testament ever published in the United States.

I have known one of these farmers, week after week, during the storms of a hard winter, drive four miles to borrow a volume of Scott's novels, and, what is better, drive four miles each week to return it. They are a people who read and think, and who can be relied on, in the long run, to take the sensible view of any question.

They have done more than read and think. They took a leading part in raising regiments and batteries for the Civil War, and their stalwart sons went valiantly forth as volunteers. The Onondaga regiments distinguished themselves on many a hard-fought field; they learned what war was like at Bull Run, and used their knowledge to good purpose at Lookout Mountain, Five Forks, and Gettysburg. Typical is the fact that one of these regiments was led by a valley schoolmaster,–a man who, having been shot through the body, reported dead, and honored with a public commemoration at which eulogies were delivered by various persons, including myself, lived to command a brigade, to take part in the "Battle of the Clouds," where he received a second wound, and to receive a third wound during the march with Sherman to the sea.

Best of all, after the war the surviving soldiers returned, went on with their accustomed vocations, and all was quiet as before.

But in the autumn [1] of 1869 this peaceful region was in commotion from one end to the other. Strange reports echoed from farm to farm. It was noised abroad that a great stone statue or petrified giant had been dug up near the little hamlet of Cardiff, almost at the southern extremity of the valley; and soon, despite the fact that the crops were

The American Goliah

not yet gathered in, and the elections not yet over, men and women and children were hurrying from Syracuse and from the farm-houses along the valley to the scene of the great discovery.

I had been absent in a distant State for some weeks, and, on my return to Syracuse, meeting one of the most substantial citizens, a highly respected deacon in the Presbyterian Church, formerly a county judge, I asked him, in a jocose way, about the new object of interest, fully expecting that he would join me in a laugh over the whole matter; but, to my surprise, he became at once very solemn. He said, "I assure you that this is no laughing matter; it is a very serious thing, indeed; there is no question that an amazing discovery has been made, and I advise you to go down and see what you think of it."

Next morning, my brother and myself were speeding, after a fast trotter in a light buggy, through the valley to the scene of the discovery; and as we went we saw more and more, on every side, evidences of enormous popular interest. The roads were crowded with buggies, carriages, and even omnibuses from the city, and with lumber-wagons from the farms–all laden with passengers. In about two hours we arrived at the Newell farm and found a gathering which at first sight seemed like a county fair. In the midst was a tent, and a crowd was pressing for admission. Entering, we saw a large pit or grave, and, at the bottom of it, perhaps five feet below the surface, an enormous figure, apparently of Onondaga gray limestone. It was a stone giant, with massive features, the whole body nude, the limbs contracted as if in agony. It had a color as if it had lain long in the earth, and over its surface were minute punctures, like pores. An especial appearance of great age was given it by deep grooves and channels in its under side, apparently worn by the water which flowed in streams through the earth and along the rock on which the figure rested. Lying in its grave, with the subdued light from the roof of the tent falling upon it, and with the limbs contorted as if in a death struggle, it produced a most weird effect. An air of great solemnity pervaded the place. Visitors hardly spoke above a whisper.

Coming out, I asked some questions, and was told that the farmer who lived there had discovered the figure when digging a well. Being asked my opinion, my answer was that the whole matter was undoubtedly a hoax; that there was no reason why the farmer should dig a well in the spot where the figure was found; that it was convenient neither to the house nor to the barn; that there was already a good spring and a stream of water running conveniently to both; that, as to the figure itself, it certainly could not have been carved by any prehistoric race, since no part of it showed the characteristics of any such early work; that, rude as it was, it betrayed the qualities of a modern performance of a low order.

Nor could it be a fossilized human being; in this all scientific observers of any note agreed. There was ample evidence, to one who had seen much sculpture, that it was carved, and that the man who carved it, though by no means possessed of genius or talent, had seen casts, engravings, or photographs of noted sculptures. The figure, in size, in massiveness, in the drawing up of the limbs, and in its roughened surface, vaguely reminded one of Michelangelo's "Night and Morning." Of course, the difference between this crude figure and those great Medicean statues was infinite; and yet it seemed to me that the man who had carved this figure must have received a hint from those.

It was also clear that the figure was neither intended to be considered as an idol nor as a monumental statue. There was no pedestal of any sort on which it could stand, and the disposition of

The American Goliah

the limbs and their contortions were not such as any sculptor would dream of in a figure to be set up for adoration. That it was intended to be taken as a fossilized giant was indicated by the fact that it was made as nearly like a human being as the limited powers of the stone-carver permitted, and that it was covered with minute imitations of pores.

Therefore it was that, in spite of all scientific reasons to the contrary, the work was very generally accepted as a petrified human being of colossal size, and became known as "the Cardiff Giant."

One thing seemed to argue strongly in favor of its antiquity, and I felt bound to confess, to those who asked my opinion, that it puzzled me. This was the fact that the surface water flowing beneath it in its grave seemed to have deeply grooved and channeled it on the under side. Now the Onondaga gray limestone is hard and substantial, and on that very account used in the locks upon the canals: for the running of surface water to wear such channels in it would require centuries.

BUST OF THE CARDIFF GIANT.

Against the opinion that the figure was a hoax various arguments were used. It was insisted, first, that the farmer had not the ability to devise such a fraud; secondly, that he had not the means to execute it; third, that his family had lived there steadily for many years, and were ready to declare under oath that they had never seen it, and had known nothing of it until it was accidentally discovered; fourth, that the neighbors had never seen or heard of it; fifth, that it was preposterous to suppose that such a mass of stone could have been brought and buried in the place without some one finding it out; sixth, that the grooves and channels worn in it by the surface water proved its vast antiquity.

To these considerations others were soon added. Especially interesting was it to observe the evolution of myth and legend. Within a week after the discovery, full-blown statements appeared to the effect that the neighboring Indians had abundant traditions of giants who formerly roamed over the hills of Onondaga; and, finally, the circumstantial story was evolved that an Onondaga squaw had declared, "in an impressive manner," that the statue "is undoubtedly the petrified body of a gigantic Indian prophet who flourished many centuries ago and foretold the coming of the palefaces, and who, just before his own death, said to those about him that their descendants would see him again." [2] To this were added the reflections of many good people who found it an edifying confirmation of the biblical text, "There were giants in those days." There was, indeed, as undercurrent of skepticism among the harder heads in the valley, but the prevailing opinion in the region at large was more and more in favor of the idea that the object was a fossilized human being–a giant of "those days." Such was the rush to see the figure that the admission receipts were very large: it was even stated that they amounted to five per cent upon three millions of dollars, and soon came active men from the neighboring region who proposed to purchase the figure and exhibit it through the country. A leading spirit in this "syndicate" deserves mention. He was a horse-dealer in a large way and banker in a small way from a village in the next county,–a man keen and shrewd, but merciful and kindly, who had fought his way up from abject poverty, and whose fundamental principle, as he asserted it, was "Do unto others as they would like to do unto you, and–*do it fust*. [3] A joint-stock concern was formed with a considerable capital, and an eminent showman, "Colonel" Wood, employed to exploit the wonder.

A week after my first visit I again went to the place, by invitation. In the crowd on that day were many men of light and leading from neighboring towns,–among them some who made pretensions to scientific knowledge. The figure, lying in its grave, deeply impressed all; and as a party of us came away, a very excellent doctor of divinity, pastor of one of the largest churches in Syracuse, said very impressively, "Is it not strange that any human being, after seeing this wonderfully preserved figure, can deny the evidence of his senses, and refuse to believe, what is so evidently the fact, that we have here a fossilized human being, perhaps one of the giants mentioned in Scripture?"

The American Goliah

Another visitor, a bright-looking lady, was heard to declare, "Nothing in the world can ever make me believe that he was not once a living being. Why, you can see the veins in his legs." [4]

Another prominent clergyman declared with *ex cathedra* emphasis: "This is not a thing contrived of man, but is the face of one who lived on the earth, the very image and child of God." [5] And a writer in one of the most important daily papers of the region dwelt on the "majestic simplicity and grandeur of the figure," and added, "It is not unsafe to affirm that ninety-nine out of every hundred persons who have seen this wonder have become immediately and instantly impressed with the idea that they were in the presence of an object not made by mortal hands.... No piece of sculpture ever produced the awe inspired by this blackened form.... I venture to affirm that no living sculptor can be produced who will say that the figure was conceived and executed by any human being." [6]

The American Goliah

The current of belief ran more and more strongly, and soon embraced a large number of really thoughtful people. A week or two after my first visit came a deputation of regents of the State University from Albany, including especially Dr. Woolworth, the secretary, a man of large educational experience, and no less a personage in the scientific world than Dr. James Hall, the State geologist, perhaps the most eminent American paleontologist of that period.

On their arrival at Syracuse in the evening, I met them at their hotel and discussed with them the subject which so interested us all, urging them especially to be cautious and stating that a mistake might prove very injurious to the reputation of the regents, and to the proper standing of scientific men and methods in the state, that if the matter should turn out to be a fraud, and such eminent authorities should be found to have committed themselves to it, there would be a guffaw from one end of the country to the other at the expense of the men intrusted by the State with its scientific and educational interests. To this the gentlemen assented, and next day they went to Cardiff. They came; they saw; and they narrowly escaped being conquered. Luckily they did not give their sanction to the idea that the statue was a petrifaction, but Professor Hall was induced to say: "To all appearance, the statue lay upon the gravel when the deposition of the fine silt or soil began, upon the surface of which the forests have grown for succeeding generations. Altogether it is the most remarkable object brought to light in this country, and, although not dating back to the stone age, is, nevertheless, deserving of the attention of

THE GREAT CARDIFF GIANT!

Discovered at Cardiff, Onondaga Co., N. Y., is now on Exhibition in the

Geological Hall, Albany,

For a few days only.

HIS DIMENSIONS.

Length of Body,	10 feet, 4 1-2 inches.
Length of Head from Chin to Top of Head,	21 "
Length of Nose,	6 "
Across the Nostrils,	3 1-2 "
Width of Mouth,	5 "
Circumference of Neck,	37 "
Shoulders, from point to point,	3 feet, 1 1-2 "
Length of Right Arm,	4 feet, 9 1-2 "
Across the Wrist,	5 "
Across the Palm of Hand,	7 "
Length of Second Finger,	8 "
Around the Thighs,	6 feet, 3 1-2 "
Diameter of the Thigh,	13 "
Through the Calf of Leg,	9 1-2 "
Length of Foot,	21 "
Across the Ball of Foot,	8 "
Weight,	2990 pounds.

ALBANY, November 19th, 1869.

The American Goliah

archaeologists. [7]

At no period of my life have I ever been more discouraged as regards the possibility of making right reason prevail among men.

As a refrain to every argument there seemed to go jeering and sneering through my brain Schiller's famous line:

"Against stupidity the gods themselves fight in vain." [8]

There seemed no possibility even of suspending the judgment of the great majority who saw the statue. As a rule, they insisted on believing It a "petrified giant," and those who did not dwelt on its perfections as an ancient statue. They saw in it a whole catalogue of fine qualities; and one writer went into such extreme ecstatics that he suddenly realized the fact, and ended by saying, "but this is rather too high-flown, so I had better conclude." As a matter of fact, the work was wretchedly defective in proportion and features; in every characteristic of sculpture it showed itself the work simply of an inferior stone-carver.

Dr. Boynton, a local lecturer on scientific subjects, gave it the highest praise as a work of art, and attributed it to early Jesuit missionaries who had come into that region about two hundred years before. Another gentleman, who united the character of a deservedly beloved pastor and an inspiring popular lecturer on various scientific topics, developed this Boynton theory. He attributed the statue to "a trained sculptor... who had noble original powers; for none but such could have formed and wrought out the conception of that stately head with its calm smile so full of mingled sweetness and strength." This writer then ventured the query, "Was it not, as Dr. Boynton suggests, some one from that French colony,... someone with a righteous soul sighing over the lost civilization of Europe, weary of swamp and forest and fort, who, finding this block by the side of the stream, solaced the weary days of exile with pouring out his thought upon the stone?" [9] Although the most eminent sculptor in the State has utterly refused to pronounce the figure anything beyond a poor piece of carving, these strains of admiration and adoration continued.

The American Goliah

There was evidently a "joy in believing" in the marvel, and this was increased by the peculiarly American superstition that the correctness of a belief is decided by the number of people who can be induced to adopt it–that truth is a matter of majorities. The current of credulity seemed irresistible.

Shortly afterward the statue was raised from its grave, taken to Syracuse and to various other cities, especially to the city of New York, and in each place exhibited as a show.

As already stated, there was but one thing in the figure, as I had seen it, which puzzled me, and that was the grooving of the under side, apparently by currents of water, which, as the statue appeared to be of our Onondaga gray limestone, would require very many years. But one day one of the cool-headed skeptics of the valley, an old schoolmate of mine, came to me, and with an air of great solemnity took from his pocket an object which he carefully unrolled from its wrappings, and said, "There is a piece of the giant. Careful guard has been kept from the first in order to prevent people touching it; but I have managed to get a piece of it, and here it is." I took it in my hand, and the matter was made clear in an instant. The stone was not our hard Onondaga gray limestone, but soft, easily marked with the finger-nail, and, on testing it with an acid, I found it, not hard carbonate of lime, but a soft, friable sulphate of lime–a form of gypsum, which must have been brought from some other part of the country.

A healthful skepticism now began to assert its rights. Professor Marsh of Yale appeared upon the scene. Fortunately, he was not only one of the most eminent of living paleontologists, but, unlike most who had given an opinion, he really knew something of sculpture, for he had been familiar with the best galleries of the Old World. He examined the statue and said, "It is of very recent origin, and a most decided humbug.... Very short exposure of the statue would suffice to obliterate all trace of tool-marks, and also to roughen the polished surfaces, but these are still quite perfect, and hence the giant must have been very recently buried.... I am surprised that any scientific observers should not have at once detected the unmistakable evidence against its antiquity." [10]

The American Goliah

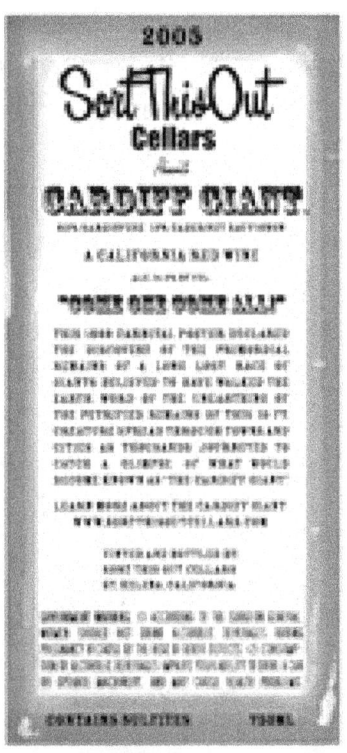

Various suspicious circumstances presently became known. It was found that Farmer Newell had just remitted to a man named Hull, at some place in the West, several thousand dollars, the result of admission fees to the booth containing the figure, and that nothing had come in return. Thinking men in the neighborhood reasoned that as Newell had never been in condition to owe any human being such an amount of money, and had received nothing in return for it, his correspondent had, not unlikely, something to do with the statue.

These suspicions were soon confirmed. The neighboring farmers, who, in their quiet way, kept their eyes open, noted a tall, lank individual who frequently visited the place and seemed to exercise complete control over Farmer Newell. Soon it was learned that this stranger was the man Hull,–Newell's brother-in-law,–the same to whom the latter had made the large remittance of admission money. One day, two or three farmers from a distance, visiting the place for the first time and seeing Hull, said, "Why, that is the man who brought the big box down the valley." On being asked what they meant, they said that, being one evening in a tavern on the valley turnpike some miles South of Cardiff, they had noticed under the tavern shed a wagon bearing an enormous box; and when they met

The American Goliah

Hull in the bar-room and asked about it, he said that it was some tobacco-cutting machinery which he was bringing to Syracuse. Other farmers, who had seen the box and talked with Hull at different places on the road between Binghamton and Cardiff, made similar statements. It was then ascertained that no such box had passed the toll-gates between Cardiff and Syracuse, and proofs of the swindle began to mature. But skepticism was not well received. Vested interests had accrued, a considerable number of people, most of them very good people, had taken stock in the new enterprise, and anything which discredited it was unwelcome to them.

THE PETRIFIED MAN.

NOW, to show how really hard it is to foist a moral or a truth upon an unsuspecting public through a burlesque without entirely and absurdly missing one's mark, I will here set down two experiences of my own in this thing. In the fall of 1862, in Nevada and California, the people got to running wild about extraordinary petrifications and other natural marvels. One could scarcely pick up a paper without finding in it one or two glorified discoveries of this

The American Goliah

It was not at all that these excellent people wished to countenance an imposture, but it had become so entwined with their beliefs and their interests that at last they came to abhor any doubts regarding it. A pamphlet, "The American Goliath," was now issued in behalf of the wonder. On its title-page it claimed to give the "History of the Discovery, and the Opinions of Scientific Men thereon." The tone of the book was moderate, but its tendency was evident. Only letters and newspaper articles exciting curiosity or favoring the genuineness of the statue were admitted; adverse testimony, like that of Professor Marsh, was carefully excluded.

Before long the matter entered into a comical phase. Barnum, King of Showmen, attempted to purchase the "giant," but in vain. He then had a copy made so nearly resembling the original that no one, save, possibly, an expert, could distinguish between them. This new statue was also exhibited as "the Cardiff Giant," and thenceforward the credit of the discovery waned.

The catastrophe now approached rapidly, and soon affidavits from men of high character in Iowa and Illinois established the fact that the figure was made at Fort Dodge, in Iowa, of a great block of gypsum there found; that this block was transported by land to the nearest railway station, Boone, which was about forty-five miles distant; that on the way the wagon conveying it broke down, and that as no other could be found strong enough to bear the whole weight, a portion of the block was cut off; that, thus diminished, it was taken to Chicago, where a German stone-carver gave it final shape; that, as it had been shortened, he was obliged to draw up the lower limbs, thus giving it a strikingly contracted and agonized appearance; that the under side of the figure was grooved and channeled in order that it should appear to be wasted by age; that it was then dotted or pitted over with minute pores by means of a leaden mallet faced with steel needles; that it was stained with some preparation which gave it an appearance of great age; that it was then shipped to a place near Binghamton, New York, and finally brought to Cardiff and there buried. It was further stated that Hull, in order to secure his brother-in-law, Farmer Newell, as his confederate in burying the statue, had sworn him to secrecy; and, in order that the family might testify that they had never heard or seen anything of the statue until it had been unearthed, he had sent them away on a little excursion covering the time when it was brought and buried. All these facts were established by affidavits from men of high character in Iowa and Illinois, by the sworn testimony of various Onondaga farmers and men of business, and, finally, by the admissions and even boasts of Hull himself.

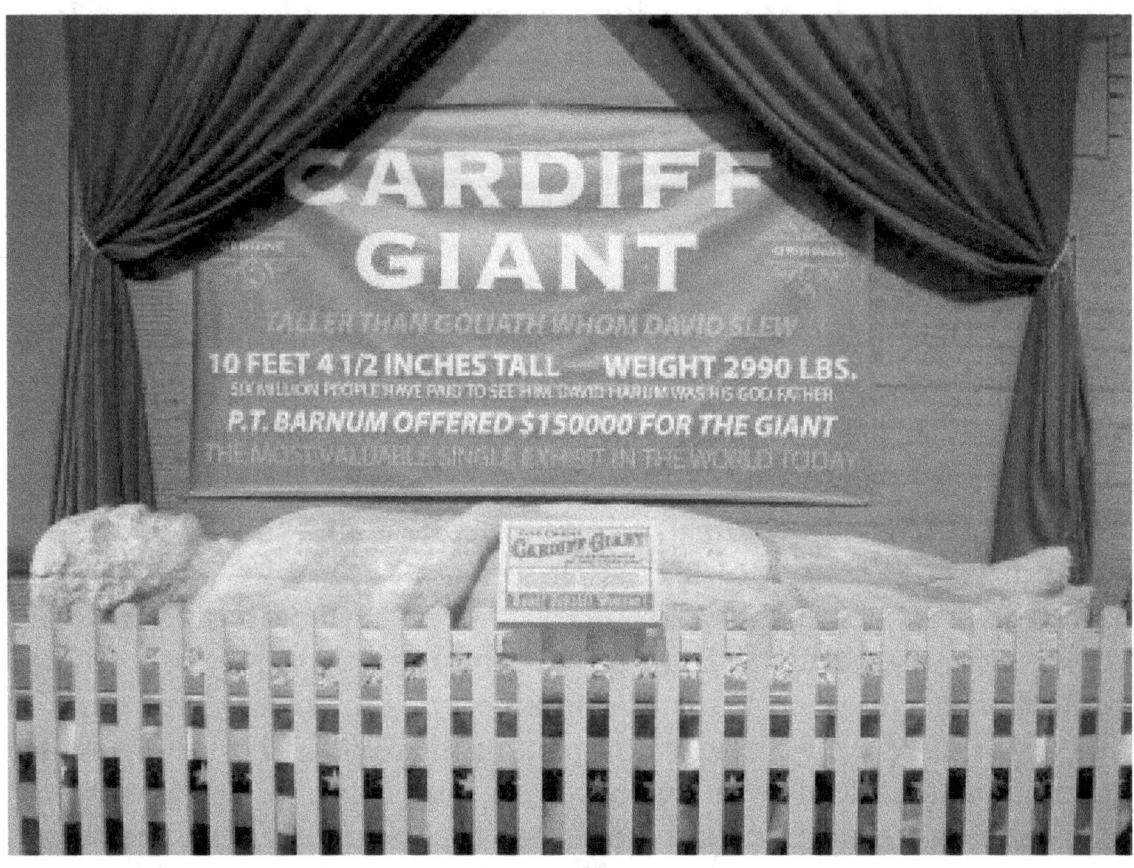

Against this tide of truth the good people who had pinned their faith to the statue–those who had vested interests in it, and those who had rashly given solemn opinions in favor of it–struggled for a time desperately. A writer in the "Syracuse Journal" expressed a sort of regretful wonder and shame that "the public are asked to overthrow the sworn testimony of sustained witnesses corroborated by the highest scientific authorities–the only sworn witness being Farmer Newell, whose testimony was not at all conclusive, and the highest scientific authority being an eminent local dentist who, early in his life, had given popular chemical lectures, and who had now invested money in the enterprise.

The same writer referred also with awe to "the men of sense, property, and character who own the giant and receive whatever revenue arises from its exhibition"; and the argument culminated in the oracular declaration that "the operations of water as testified and interpreted by science cannot create falsehood." [11]

But all this pathetic eloquence was in vain. Hull, the inventor of the statue, having realized more money from it than he expected, and being sharp enough to see that its day was done, was evidently bursting with the desire to avert scorn from himself by bringing the laugh upon others, and especially upon certain clergymen, whom, as we shall see hereafter, he greatly disliked. He now acknowledged that the whole thing was a swindle, and gave details of the way in which he came to embark in it. He avowed that the idea was suggested to him by a discussion with a Methodist revivalist in Iowa; that, being himself a skeptic in religious matters, he had flung at his antagonist "those remarkable stories in the Bible about giants"; that, observing how readily the revivalist and those with him took up the cudgels for the giants, it then and there occurred to him that, since so many people found pleasure in believing such things, he would have a statue carved out of stone which he had found in Iowa and pass it off on them as a petrified giant. In a later conversation he said that one thing which decided him was that the stone had in it dark-colored bluish streaks which resembled in appearance the veins of the human body. The evolution of the whole affair thus became clear, simple, and natural.

Up to this time, Hull's remarkable cunning had never availed him much. He had made various petty inventions, but had realized very little from them; he had then made some combinations as regarded the internal-revenue laws referring to the manufacture and sale of tobacco, and these had only brought him into trouble with the courts; but now, when the boundless resources of human credulity were suddenly revealed to him by the revivalist, he determined to exploit them. This evolution of his ideas strikingly resembles that through which the mind of a worthless, shiftless, tricky creature in western New York–Joseph Smith–must have passed forty years before, when he dug up "the golden plates" of the "Book of Mormon," and found plenty of excellent people who rejoiced in believing that the Rev. Mr. Spalding's biblical novel was a new revelation from the Almighty.

The American Goliah

The whole matter was thus fully laid open, and it might have been reasonably expected that thenceforward no human being would insist that the stone figure was anything but a swindling hoax.

Not so. In the Divinity School of Yale College, about the middle of the century, was a solemn, quiet, semi-jocose, semi-melancholic resident graduate–Alexander McWhorter. I knew him well. He had embarked in various matters which had not turned out satisfactorily. Hot water, ecclesiastical and social, seemed his favorite element. [12] He was generally believed to secure most of his sleep during the day, and to do most of his work during the night; a favorite object of his study being Hebrew. Various strange things had appeared from his pen, and, most curious of all, a little book entitled, "Yahveh Christ," in which he had endeavored to demonstrate that the doctrine of the Trinity was to be found entangled in the consonants out of which former scholars made the word "Jehovah," and more recent scholars "Yahveh"; that this word, in fact, proved the doctrine of the Trinity. [13]

He now brought his intellect to bear upon "the Cardiff Giant," and soon produced an amazing theory, developing it at length in a careful article. [14]

This theory was simply that the figure discovered at Cardiff was a Phenician idol; and Mr. McWhorter published, as the climax to all his proofs, the facsimile and translation of an inscription which he had discovered upon the figure–a "Phenician inscription which he thought could leave no doubt in the mind of any person open to conviction.

That the whole thing had been confessed a swindle by all who took part in it, with full details as to its origin and development, seemed to him not worthy of the slightest mention. Regardless of all the facts in the case, he showed a pathetic devotion to his theory, and allowed his imagination the fullest play. He found, first of all, an inscription of thirteen letters, introduced by a large cross or star–the Assyrian index of the Deity." Before the last word of the inscription he found carved "a flower which he regarded as consecrated to the particular deity Tammuz, and at both ends of the inscription a serpent monogram and symbol of Baal."

This inscription he assumed as an evident fact, though no other human being had ever been able to see it. Even Professor White M.D., of the Yale Medical School, with the best intentions in the world, was unable to find it. Dr. White was certainly not inclined to superficiality or skepticism. With "achromatic glasses which magnified forty-five diameters he examined the "pinholes" which covered the figure, and declared that "the beautiful finish of every pore or pinhole appeared to me strongly opposed to the idea that the statue was of modern workmanship." He also thought he saw the markings which Mr. McWhorter conjectured might be an inscription, and said in a letter, "though I saw no recent tool-marks, I saw evidences of design in the form and arrangement of the markings, which suggested the idea of an inscription. And, finally, having made these concessions, he ends his long letter with the very guarded statement that," though not fully decided, I incline to the opinion that the Onondaga statue is of ancient origin." [18]

But this mild statement did not daunt Mr. McWhorter. Having calmly pronounced Dr. White "in error," he proceeded with sublime disregard of every other human being. He found that the statue "belongs to the winged or `cherubim' type"; that "down the left side of the figure are seen the outlines of folded wings—even the separate feathers being clearly distinguishable"; that "the left side of the head is inexpressibly noble and majestic." and "conforms remarkably to the type of the head of the mound-builders"; that "the left arm terminates in what appears to be a huge extended lion's paw"; that "the dual idea expressed in the head is carried out in the figure"; that "in the wonderfully artistic mouth of the divine side we find a suggestion of that of the Greek Apollo." Mr. McWhorter also found other things that no other human being was ever able to discern, and among them " a crescent-shaped wound upon the left side," "traces of ancient coloring" in all parts of the statue, and evidences that the minute pores were made by "borers." He lays great stress on an "ancient medal" found in Onondaga, which he thinks belongs "to the era of the mound-builders," and on which he finds a "circle inclosing an equilateral cross, both cross and circle, like the wheel of Ezekiel, being full of small circles or eyes." As a matter of fact, this "ancient medal" was an English penny, which a street gamin of Syracuse said that he had found near the statue, and the "equilateral cross" was simply the usual cross of St. George. Mr. McWhorter thinks the circle inclosing the cross denotes the "world soul" and in a dissertation of about twenty pages he discourses upon "Baal," "Tammuz," "King Hiram of Tyre," the "ships of Tarshish," the "Eluli," and "Atlas," with plentiful arguments drawn from a multitude of authorities, and among them Sanchoniathon, Ezekiel, Plato, Dr. Döllinger, Isaiah, Melanchthon, Lenormant, Humboldt, Sir John Lubbock, and Don Domingo Juarros,–finally satisfying himself that the statue was "brought over by a colony of Phenicians," possibly several hundred years before Christ. [16]

With the modesty of a true scholar he says, "Whether the final battle at Onondaga... occurred before or after this event we cannot tell"; but, resuming confidence, he says, "we only know that at some distant period the great statue, brought in a `ship of Tarshish' across the sea of Atl, was lightly covered with twigs and flowers, and these with gravel." The deliberations of the Pickwick Club over "Bill Stubbs, His Mark" pale before this; and Dickens in his most expansive moods never conceived anything more funny than the long, solemn discussion between the erratic Hebrew scholar and the eminent medical professor at New Haven over the "pores" of the statue, which one of them thought "the work of minute animals," which the other thought "elaborate Phenician workmanship," which both thought exquisite, and which the maker of the statue had already confessed that he had made by rudely striking the statue with a mallet faced with needles. Mr. McWhorter's new theory made no great stir in the United States, though some, doubtless, took comfort in it; but it found one very eminent convert across the ocean, and in a place where we might least have expected him. Some ten years after the events above sketched, while residing at Berlin as minister of the United States, I one day received from an American student at the University of Halle a letter stating that he had been requested by no less a personage than the eminent Dr Schlottmann, instructor in Hebrew in the theological School of that university,–the successor of Gesenius in that branch of instruction,–to write me for information regarding the Phenician statue described by the Rev. Alexander McWhorter.

The American Goliah

In reply, I detailed to him the main points in the history of the case, as it has been given in this chapter, adding, as against the Phenician theory, that nothing in the nature of Phenician remains had ever been found within the borders of the United States, and that if

The American Goliah

they had been found, this remote valley, three hundred miles from the Seas barred from the coast by mountain-ranges, forests, and savage tribes, could never have been the place chosen by Phenician navigators for such a deposit; that the figure itself was clearly not a work of early art, but a crude development by an uncultured stone-cutter out of his remembrance of things in modern sculpture; and that the inscription was purely the creation of Mr. McWhorter's imagination.

In his acknowledgment, my correspondent said that I had left no doubt in his mind as to the fact that the giant was a swindle; but that he had communicated my letter to the eminent Dr. Schlottmann, that the later avowed that I had not convinced him, and that he still believed the Cardiff figure to be a Phenician statue bearing a most important inscription. One man emerged from this chapter in the history of human folly supremely happy: this was Hull, the inventor of the "giant." He had at last made some money, had gained a reputation for "smartness," and, what probably pleased him best of all, had revenged himself upon the Rev. Mr. Turk of Ackley, Iowa, who by lungpower had worsted him in the argument as to the giants mentioned in Scripture.

So elate was he that he shortly set about devising another "petrified man" which would defy the world. It was of clay baked in a furnace, contained human bones, and was provided with "a tail and legs of the ape type"; and this he caused to be buried and discovered in Colorado. This time he claimed to have the aid of one of his former foes–the great Barnum; and all went well until his old enemy, Professor Marsh of Yale, appeared and blasted the whole enterprise by a few minutes of scientific observation and common-sense discourse.

Others tried to imitate Hull, and in 1876 one–William Ruddock of Thornton, St. Clair County, Michigan–manufactured a small effigy in cement, and in due time brought about the discovery of it. But, though several country clergymen used it to strengthen their arguments as to the literal, prosaic correctness of Genesis, it proved a failure. Finally, in 1889, twenty years after "the Cardiff Giant" was devised, a "petrified man" was found near Bathurst in Australia, brought to Sydney, and exhibited. The result was, in some measure,

The American Goliah

the same as in the case of the American fraud. Excellent people found comfort in believing, and sundry pseudo-scientific men of a cheap sort thought it best to pander to this sentiment; but a self-trained geologist pointed out the absurdity of the popular theory, and finally the police finished the matter by securing evidences of fraud. [17]

To close these annals, I may add that recently the inventor of "the Cardiff Giant," Hull, being at the age of seventy-six years, apparently in his last illness, and anxious for the glory in history which comes from successful achievement, again gave to the press a full account of his part in the affair, confirming what he had previously stated, showing how he planned it, executed it, and realized a goodly sum for it; how Barnum wished to purchase it from him; and how, above all, he had his joke at the expense of those who, though they had managed to overcome him in argument, had finally been rendered ridiculous in the sight of the whole country.[18]

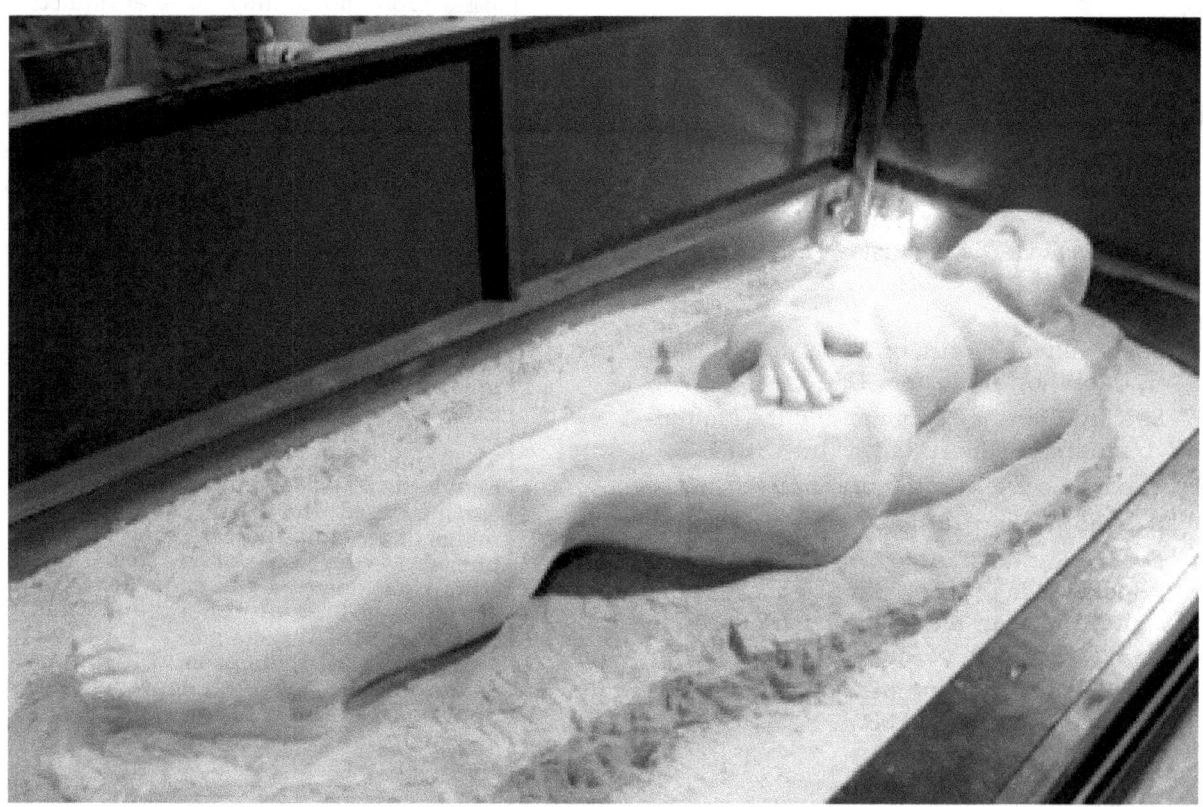

Endnotes

[1] October 16.

[2] See "The Cardiff Giant Humbug," Fort Dodge, Iowa, 1870, p.13.

[3] For a picture, both amusing and pathetic, of the doings of this man, and also of life in the central Now York villages, see "David Harum," a novel by E. N. Westcott, New York, 1898.

[4] See Letter of Hon. Galusha Parsons in the Fort Dodge Pamphlet.

[5] See Mr. Stockbridge's article in the "Popular Science Monthly," June, 1878.

[6] See "The American Goliath," Syracuse, 1869, p. 16.

[7] See his letter of October 23, 1869, in the Syracuse papers.

[8] "Mit der Dummheit kämpfen Götter selbst vergebens." *Jungfrau von Orleans,* Act III, scene 6.

[9] See the Syracuse daily papers as above.

[10] See Professor Marsh's letter in the "Syracuse Daily Journal," November 30, 1869.

[11] See letter of "X" in the "Syracuse Journal," republished in the Fort Dodge Pamphlet, pp. 15 and 16.

[12] The main evidence of this is to be found in "Truth Stranger Than Fiction: A Narrative of Recent Transactions involving Inquiries in Regard to the Principles of Honor, Truth, and Justice, which Obtains in a Distinguished American University," by Catherine E. Beecher, New York, 1850.

[13] See: "Yahveh Christ, or the Memorial Name," by A. McWhorter, Boston, 1857.

[14] See McWhorter, "Tammuz and the Moundbuilders," in the "Galaxy," July, 1872.

[15] The italics are as in the original.

[16] See the "Galaxy" article, as above, *passim.*

[17] For the Ruddock discovery see Dr. G. A. Stockwell in the "Popular Science Monthly" for June, 1878. For the Australian fraud see the London "Times" of August 2, 1889.

[18] For Hull's "Final Statement" see the "Ithaca Daily Journal," January 4, 1898.

Another Cardiff Giant—As It Were.

An Image of a Man Found in Taughanock Ravine, Tompkins County—Is it a Petrefaction, or is it a Fraud?

From the Elmira Advertiser.

TRUMANSBURG, July 4.

TO THE EDITOR OF THE ADVERTISER: Taughanock ravine has disgorged a specimen of the *genus homo* which seems to savor of the long-forgotten past. A man who sported one club-foot and one other which was inconveniently long, has been torn from his resting place and lies exposed to the mercy of sight-seers who have the curiosity and the necessary cash. His stately form when in life must have towered up towards the stars at least six feet and one-half. The length in its present position is six feet and two inches. The shoulders are twenty inches broad.

Dr. Congdon, formerly of the Binghampton Inebriate Asylum, and many other professional men, have examined the specimen to-day. No one seems willing to express an opinion about the matter, and in fact the mystery is great. If it is not a genuine petrefaction, it is certainly an excellant fraud. The circumstances attending its discovery are perfectly natural, and to all appearances there is no bad faith about it. The hands are crossed at the wrists and the left leg crosses the right midway below the knee. The appearance of the body leads to the belief that the individual was on earth before our present civilization and must have belonged to a people now extinct. His remains were discovered by the roadside on the north bank of Taghanic ravine and some distance above the Falls. About three feet of earth covered the body, and the remains of a stump indicate that he was buried at the foot of a tree. The stump was decayed and gone clear below the surface of the ground, and only a trace of it remains.

Mr. John M. Thompson, the owner of the "fossil," has been improving the upper part of the glen for some time, and workmen in his employ found the specimen.

The Cuba Patriot, Cuba NY
July 11, 1879

The American Goliah

THE AMERICAN GOLIAH.

A WONDERFUL

Geological Discovery.

A PETRIFIED GIANT,

TEN AND ONE-HALF FEET HIGH, DISCOVERED IN ONONDAGA COUNTY, N. Y.

HISTORY OF THE DISCOVERY ON OCTOBER 16, 1869, OF AN IMAGE OF STONE, THE SAME BEING A PERFECTLY FORMED AND WELL DEVELOPED MAN. DESCRIPTIONS OF THE PETRIFACTION, WITH

The Opinions of Scientific Men thereon.

From a handbill advertising the Giant

The American Goliah

From a handbill advertising the Giant

The American Goliah

Back a few years ago we presented California key UFOlogist Sean Casteel with an assignment to cull through the works of researcher Harold T. Wilkins who had written on a variety of topics in the 1950s from tales of UFOs, treasure hunting pirates, Atlantis, to lost continents, to giant sized beings and creatures of all types. What resulted was a cleverly crafted book - *UFO ATTACK EARTH: ACCOMPANIED BY WARRIORS FROM ATLANTIS, LOST CITIES, LIVING DINOSAURS, AND A BLOODY ARSED PIRATE OR TWO.* For the purposes of this volume we have reassigned some of the pages in the Casteel-Wilkins work that have the most to do with our consideration of all things gigantic and humongous still appearing upon the earth from time to time.

Strange Creatures and Monsters Galore
by
Harold T. Wilkins

One of the most fascinating phases in the career of Harold T. Wilkins came in the latter part of the 1940s when he produced an intriguing monograph called *Monsters and Mysteries of America, the Jungles, the Tropics, and the Arctic Wastes.* The subtitle of this rather condensed—and certainly straightforward—tome is *Strange Stories of Modern Adventures Suggesting That The King Kongs And The Dinosaurs May Still Be Alive Today.* Not only is that a whopper of a title—even longer than the one given to this contemporary edition showcasing his literary skills—but it makes by far the most exaggerated claims to be found in any of Wilkins' work. It appears as we flip through the pages that Wilkins has donned a professor's cap and a detective's spyglass, a la Indiana Jones, and has taken to the rugged back roads and dense jungles twisted with impenetrable vines in search of beasts long thought to have dissolved into time.

Tall Tales Versus Scientific Skepticism

It is possible that in remote and still unexplored regions of the earth, in the depths of the seas and far-ranging oceans, monsters and strange forms of life exist which are unknown to, and therefore unclassified, by scientists and natural historians, or oceanographical museum experts?

Palaeontologists are apt to smile at such a question as being absurd. They will point out that such phenomena as the ice ages, or the glaciation of the climate over thousands of years—which north and south of the equator, followed life's long summer on earth, when gigantic saurians wallowed in the slime of the warm beaches of shallower seas and dinosaurs ranged a much lower land—exterminated all such genera and species. Marine biologists, too, usually scout the idea that there may still exist in the great depths of the oceans, or in the mid-deeps, any such monsters as "sea serpents." They ask us to name any oceanographical museum or marine biological institute of research which possesses a bone of such creatures.

However, in this latter connection, I happen to possess photographs of monstrous-shaped and sized skulls and vertebrae in private collections. I can quote from the logs of a modern British warship, and the journal of a German submarine commander in the First World War, who, after torpedoing and watching the sinking, in the mid-Atlantic, of a British freighter, witnessed the throwing up from the depths a monstrous sea saurian unknown to marine biology. This should warn against dogmatism on such matters. It is also a fact that more of these events might be entered in the logs of British warships were it not for the fact that their lordships of the British Board of Admiralty are apt to cast a malign eye on the prospects of promotion of any officer who enters such an event in his log or journal.

On land, the wild animal trapper, out "to bring 'em back alive" from the jungles and bush of Africa or Asia says, with a skeptical smile, that it is not unknown for Negroes in regions remote from the confines of civilization to tell stories of strange animals and fearsome monsters in lone and unexplored forests and jungles which have never been seen by a white man. The trapper adds that if he were to let such stories divert him from the main trail of his safari, he would never bring anything back alive—save a reputation for naïve credulity, which would prejudice him in the eyes of directors of zoological parks, or wild animal dealers.

Plateaux Of Western U.S. And "Lost World" Of Brazil

And yet, before we dismiss all such stories to the limbo of travelers' tales—and the "anthropophagi and men whose heads do hang beneath their shoulders"—we must bear in mind that, in old Asia, and even older North and South America, there are vast areas which have never been under sea since the Eocene Age. One of them is the 1,500,000 square mile region, still unexplored, of the Roosevelt-Govaz tableland, in central Brazil. Another is the high plateaux section of Nevada, Arizona, Colorado and Utah. This latter arid and alkaline territory is said to be one of the oldest parts of the world above sea level. The central Brazilian tableland of mysteries, bounded by the Rio Araguaya, tributary of the mighty Amazon, or Maranon, and intersected by the mostly unexplored Rios Xingu and Tapajos, (latitude 5 degrees S. to 12 degrees S., and longitude 50 degrees to 63 degrees W.) is characterized by plutonic rocks and a queer plant louse. The rocks have been formed under the influence of volcanic fires, and there are no alluvial layers denoting past submersion. The louse, called "Brazilaphis Bondari," after the Brazilian professor Bondar, of Russian origin, lives on the lowest parts of plants and any inundation would at once have exterminated this most ancient insect as it has in other parts of the world. Taken together, the two facts suggest that this strange region of Brazil and its Asiatic counterpart of Angara, in the Siberian provinces of Irkutsk and Yakutsk, where similar phenomena have been observed, may never have been under water since the azoic age.

Even the most conservative geologists who have visited the central Brazilian tableland admit that it has been above sea level for a much earlier epoch than the last glacial age.

I have mentioned this Brazilian "Lost World" at some length because the Indians of the Matto Grosso of Brazil, which lies near it, say that it has a vast belt of rivers, swamps and marshy jungles and forests, which date back to the far day of the rising of the Andes. They say that great lizards of the type of the prehistoric saurian, extinct elsewhere on the earth millions of years ago, still wallow in its swamps and emerge on the beaches of great lagoons. Later, I shall tell a story which purports that a great ape of a veritable "King Kong" type is among the fearsome inhabitants of this lost world, which was, say forest Indian traditions, the home of a white and highly civilized race who thousands of years ago ruled the Indians' ancestors.

J. Lerius Meets Monster Lizard On Island Near Rio

One of the earliest stories of an encounter with an unknown monster in the Americas occurs in the account of the travels of Jean Lerius, a Frenchman. He was one of the company of Admiral Nicolas Durand de Villegagnon, who, in 1555, attempted to found a French colony, called "Nouvelle Geneve" (New Geneva), in an island in the bay of Rio de Janeiro. It was about the year 1557, when Lerius and two other Frenchmen, who had no "hand gunnes," but "only our swords," were in a wood in the interior of Brazil.

"We had not Barbarians (Indians) to guide us, and therefore wandered in the woods and passed through a deep valley, hearing the noise of a certain beast coming towards us, supposing it to be some timorous and harmless wild beast, notwithstanding, proceeding on our intended journey, we were secure and quiet in our mind, but presently, thirty paces distant from us, on the right hand, we saw a lizard on a hill, bigger than the body of a man, and five or six feet long. He, being spread all over with white and rough scales like oyster shells, holding up one of his forefeet, with his head aloft, and staring eyes began to behold us.

"Wherefore, being astonished (for none of us, as it then fell out, carried a hand gunne, but had only our swords at our sides, and bows and arrows, which weapons could not greatly hurt that Monster, armed with such hard scales). Notwithstanding, fearing lest if we shifted ourselves by flight, being swifter than we, he would dispatch us altogether. The one fearfully beheld the other, and we stood still in the same place. But after that prodigious, fearful lizard had beheld us a quarter of an hour, with an open mouth, and because it was exceeding hot weather (for it was a clear day, almost at noon), fetching a deep groan, that we might easily hear it, upon a sudden, he went unto the top of a mountain, with so great noise of the crashing and breaking of twigs and boughs, as of a deer running through a wood which could scarce have made more noise, we, therefore, who were then much affrighted not being very careful to pursue him, gave thanks to God and pursued our intended journey. And embracing their opinion, who affirm that the lizard is delighted with the sight of man, it seemed to me that the beholding of us pleased the Monster so much as we were tormented through his presence."

This adventure occurred in the country of the Tupinambas Indians. The description of Lerius does not fit the structure of the cayman, or any alligator or crocodile known to zoology, and however it may be with the quaint notion of Lerius that the monster was pleased with the sight of men, the story suggests that there was as much fear on one side as there was anything but delight on the other. It was probably lucky for the Frenchmen that they had no "hand gunnes"; for the use of such primitive matchlocks of those days would doubtless have led to the death of some of the men. In days far later than those of Lerius, roamers in the jungles of South America have found it wiser to forbear the use of weapons when suddenly encountering wild beasts, whose reaction from fear of man to fury is apt to be both sudden and fatal to the men!

Unicorns In The U.S.A.?

Our next story of an alleged encounter with a strange animal—this time, in North America—is of the believe-it-or-not sort. The monster concerned seems akin to one of those who, today, figures in the coat of arms painted on the state motorcars of King George of Buckingham Palace and Windsor Castle, England. Nevertheless, the skeptic often has a soft spot in his heart for a mystery, whether or no his intellect and powers of rationality permit him to accept such stories at their face value.

An English sailor, named David Ingram, traveled in 1568-69 from the "Rios das Minas on the Gulf of Mexico," to Cape Breton, in Accadia, or modern Nova Scotia. The story of his travels, which was an exceedingly daring trip in days when little or nothing was known of the vast stretch of territory from Florida up to what is now Maine and Nova Scotia, occurs in an exceedingly rare "Relacion," no copy of which exists in the British museum, and whose reprint in a rare book of Colonel Charles Jennett Weston, of Carolina, in 1856, would be reckoned a rare capture by a wealthy bibliophile of today.

Ingram had two other sailor pals with him and the men seem to have been castaways from some wreck off the coast of Mexico. He entered an elusive country called Norimbega, found mapped only in rare and ornamental atlases of the spouting dolphin and Princess Pocahontas vintage of the late 16th and early 17th centuries. The name seems to be a garbling of Norway, and in Andre Thevet's "Cosmographie," published in Paris, in 1575, Norimbega is located about the region covered by Massachusetts, Vermont, Maine and New Hampshire.

Says Ingram: "Our expedition did also see in those countries a Monstrous Beast, twice as big as a horse and in every proportion like unto a horse, both in mane and hooves, hair and neighing, save that it was small towards the hind parts like a greyhound. These Beasts have two teeth or horns of a foot long growing straight forth out of their nostrils. They are natural enemies of the horse. I did also see in that country both elephants and panthers, and one other strange beast bigger than a bear; yet it had neither head nor neck, and his eyes and mouth were in his breast; this beast is very ugly to behold, and cowardly of kind, yet bears a very fine skin like a rat, full of silver hair."

The Red Men Like Theirs Roasted

About 150 years later, a French explorer, Monsieur Benard de la Harpe, writing in 1719, says he found animals like those mentioned by Ingram—meaning, apparently, Unicorns!—in the country round the middle course of the Red River of Louisiana. La Harpe's expedition joined a party of Nawidishe Indians, near the confluence of the Washita and Red Rivers, then known as the False Washita, of the Indian Territory. He says that these Indians were then engaged in "roasting unicorns." La Harpe describes these beasts as about the size of a common horse, with reddish hair as long as the hair of a goat, thin legs, and single horn six inches long in the middle of the forehead. The horn did not branch out into prongs or tines. The meat was palatable.

He adds: "This description agrees well with what Monsieur de Bienville heard from the savages upon the upper Washita River, that unicorns were there to be found."

It may be noted that this usually considered fabulous animal was said by Pliny and Aristotle to be a one-horned beast as large as a horse. Also, the description does not fit that of a buffalo, or the American bison, which then, as we know, roamed the prairies.

The Giant
(by Goya)

The American Goliah

**The Cyclops Polyphemus
(by Carracci)**

Dinosaurs Haunt America

Marching through the foliage of time, we continue to excerpt from Wilkins' pint-sized monograph, which was originally published as one of the immensely popular, twenty-five cent "little-big books," advertised in **The Police Gazette** and the comic books of the day. **Monsters and Mysteries of America, the Jungles, the Tropics and the Arctic Wastes** contains fascinating accounts of strange felines terrorizing America in the 1700s. Wilkins next moves on to reports of dinosaurs seen in North America, offering up the radical perspective that perhaps man and the dinosaurs shared the Earth and were not widely separated in time, as most scientists would insist, even today. These same dinosaurs might be known to eat the odd American Indian now and then, as one story declares.

Jefferson Reports On Fossil Of Pre-Historic Feline

Now we may pass on to a remarkable story of an adventure of a hunter in Virginia who encountered a strange monster "whose roarings shook the ground, and which carried off horses as if they were sheep." (These were the words of President Jefferson.) In the American Philosophical Society's transactions of 1799, Jefferson reported that laborers, digging a cave at Greenbriar, in western Virginia, unearthed at a depth of three feet the bones of an unknown species of clawed animal. The earth was "nitrous," and the bones were those of an unguiculated (nailed or clawed) quadruped, "the lion being his nearest neighbor in size." But the monster, on the evidence of the remains in the case, must have been three times the size of a lion, or *Leo Africanus*.

"Megalonyx" Of Jefferson Encountered In The Flesh

At this date, there existed traditions that the early adventurers in the county of Greenbriar, Virginia, were alarmed at their first camp, in the night of their arrival, by the terrible roarings of some beast unknown to them. He went round and round their camp, and they saw his eyes shining like two balls of fire. So terrified were their horses, that they crouched down, trembling and sweating on the ground, while their hunting dogs crept in among them, not daring even to bark. Their campfires, it was thought, protected them; but next morning the would-be settlers packed up and quitted the country as too dangerous for men to live in, in isolated cabins.

This encounter happened about the year 1760. In 1765, two men, George Wilson and John Davies, went on a hunting trip to the Cheat River, a branch of the Monongahela, in western Virginia. One night, some way from their camp, they heard coming a tremendous roar which became louder, till it seemed like thunder, and the ground seemed to be all of a tremble with the reverberations. Whatever this animal was, it remained near their camp for a long time and appeared to be prowling around. Their dogs, normally savage animals, crept to the men's feet and would not budge an inch from the fire. They would neither quit the camp nor bark.

In a few moments, the hunters heard an answering roar from the top of a mountain about a mile off, and in a minute or two came a roar from a neighboring knob of the mountain. A Colonel John Stewart had this story from Wilson when he met him, in 1769. In the Revolutionary War, Stewart was colonel of the regiment in which Wilson was a private. He also heard the same story from Davies, who, in 1799, was living down in "ole Kaintuck." And truly, even the boys of "old Kaintuck" might have sheered off any close encounter with this monster, whom President Jefferson styled the "megalonyx."

In South Africa, so Jefferson was told, dogs behaved in the same way when large, man-eating lions were around.

Another man named Draper came to close quarters with this mysterious "megalonyx" when he was hunting along the Kanhawa in 1790. Draper turned his horse loose to graze, with a bell on his neck. Hardly had the horse got clear of a belt of wood, still within earshot, when the bell began to ring furiously and rapidly. Draper, grabbing his rifle, turned back, thinking that hostile Indians were around, but before he arrived on the spot where the bell was ringing, the horse had been half eaten up. Draper's dog, scenting the trail of a wild beast, followed hard on the scent and presently came in sight of an animal of enormous size. Draper, who was close behind the dog, was a daring hunter and crack shot, but he was so dumbfounded at the sight of so fearsome a beast, that he at once withdrew from sight and as silently as possible checked and brought off his dog. He said, afterwards, that he could recall no more of the monster than his enormous size, and that his general outlines were of the feline type. It was certainly not a panther or any animal known to him.

Old World Petroglyphs In Cave

That huge and unknown animals have existed in the far past in North America—which probably better deserves the title of old world, in both an ethnological and a zoological sense than Europe does—is suggested by a remarkable discovery made in a cave in Ohio, about 1810, at a location some 20 miles below the mouth of the Wabash. The cave is in a big rock which stands just above the water when the river is in flood. In the days of the early settlers of Ohio, the cave was a rendezvous of ruffians, robbers and high-jackers hailing from Kentucky. These outlaws terrorized all traffic up and down the river. They ravaged, plundered, and murdered over a wide territory. The gang was led by a fellow named Wilson.

Here is an account given by a little known American writer of the early 1820s:

"Wilson brought his family to the cave and fitted it up as a dwelling. He put out a sign on a board on the waterside: 'Wilson's Liquor Vault and House of Entertainment.' He organized a band of robbers and formed plans to murder crews of boats who stopped at his tavern. Then he manned the boats with his own thugs and sent them to New Orleans, where their lading was sold. The cash was conveyed by hand through the states of Tennessee and Kentucky, and on the road, the returning party were ordered to ambush and rob and murder likely men. Presently, the robbed merchants and relatives of good and respectable men, who had gone missing and were never heard of again, offered rewards. It was found that Wilson, at the head of 35 thugs, had a hide-out and observation post at Hurricane Island, where every passing boat was stopped and looted.

"He had fences and receivers at Natchez and New Orleans, and the cave was his treasure vault. The cave was entered after the Wilson gang had been rounded up. It was found to be 12 rods long and five wide, but what excited astonishment was that the cave proved to be the home, or religious center, of some ancient and unknown race. The floor was as flat as the pavement of an old cathedral in England and the sides rose in stony grades like the seats in a theater pit. On the walls had been executed glyphs of unknown animals.

"Beyond and above the cavern lay another even more gloomy cave. It was joined to it by a passage or an opening of around 14 feet, to ascend which was like passing up a chimney. Far above was the mountain. Some time after the robbers had been broken up, searchers in the upper cavern found six skeletons, but it cannot be said whether they were prehistoric or the remains of men murdered by Wilson and his gang."

On the walls of the lower cave—besides curious glyphs of the phases of the sun and moon, a panther held by his ears by a child, a buzzard tearing out the heart of a prostrate man, a crocodile, scorpions, and a curious hydra serpent—were no fewer than eight images of animals of unknown type. Three of these looked like elephants without tusks or tails, one like a toxodon, another like a tiger, and the last like a quadrumane whose claws were alike before and behind. This strange monster was depicted as in the act of conveying something to its mouth, which was located in its middle.

In passing, one may add, though it has no immediate concern with the subject of this booklet, that the cave walls bore fine and striking images of ancient clothed men and woman, by no means like Amero-Indians, but wearing rich cloaks, breeches open at the knees, sandals tied across the toes and heels, a bandeau tied with feathers encircling the head. The dress of the women resembled that of classic Greece, the hair clasped with a crown confined by a bodkin, and they had a sort of stola or gown, and a zone or cestus confining an "indusium," or female undergarment; they also were sandaled. Finally, there was a curious glyph of a serpent biting its tail, in an orb or circle, which, in the ancient world, symbolized the rotation of the earth and the planets, and the notion that matter and the world were renewed by feeding on themselves.

It is possible that this strange race were coeval with the dead cities of old Brazil, referred to above. Neither Wilson nor any member of his gang of robbers had the knowledge necessary to have faked such remarkable petroglyphs, nor any inducement or inclination to carry out such works, requiring artistic skill and a considerable degree of classic culture. In that, they resembled the old *bandeiristas* (land pirates) of Brazil who, in 1750, blundered on the ruins of a dead and extremely ancient city in the interior of Bahia province, located on the ancient Highlands of old Brazil.

A Reptile "Mosqueto" Near Syracuse; A Horned Serpent Whose Stench Could Kill

The North American Indians, from the shores of Florida, right up into the Arctic Circle, have folklore and traditions about the past existence of monsters, which are not always mere fables and fairytales of the childhood of the race.

David Cusick, in a rare pamphlet on the "History of the Six Indian Nations," published at Lewiston, N.Y., in 1828, collected from the Oneida branch of the Tuscaroras a story about a great reptile called the "Mesqueto," which invaded their ancient lands from Lake Onondaga and killed a number of people. Authentic or not, up until about 1885, tracks of some queer birdlike monster—about 20 inches long and extending for 20 rods—were to be seen near Brighton, south of Syracuse, N.Y., though it is rather suspiciously added that the Indians often renewed the track of this monster. They also have stories about a great horned serpent that appeared in Lake Ontario, "2,200 years before the time of Columbus," whose stench killed many people. This was about the time when a "blazing star," or immense aerolite fell into an Indian fort on the St. Lawrence and actually did kill off a number of the red men.

Was Early Man Coeval With Dinosaurs?

Dinosaurs of the Mesozoic Age do not seem to have left a trace of themselves in America's Tertiary rocks, says Dr. R.S. Lull, professor of vertebrate paleontology, at Yale University, in 1917. He says that the rising of the land and the draining of the great inland Cretaceous seas along the low-lying shores, where the dinosaurs had their home, spelled their doom. But the career of these immense reptilia of geologic ages was not brief. In fact, it seems to have lasted for an evolutionary period three times as long as that of the entire mammalian age. The dinosaur does not represent a futile attempt on the part of Nature to people the earth with creatures of insignificant moment. These monsters are comparable in their majestic rise, slow culmination, and dramatic fall to the greatest nations of antiquity. So says the professor.

Yet, there have been recent discoveries in U.S. territory which suggest that early man, contrary to the accepted theories of the paleontologists and evolutionists, may have been coeval with dinosaurs who managed to survive cataclysmic upheavals in other parts of the earth. Let us glance at this evidence.

A Dinosaur Idol Found At Granby, California

In 1926, a man named Jordan was digging to make a garage at a place near Granby, California. He uncovered a queer idol at a depth of 12 feet. I have a sketch of it. There were other remains that suggested that an ancient settlement had once existed nearby. But the idol was of a hard green stone like nothing known in the locality. It may have come from a long distance, for it suggests the Amazon stone or chalcuhitl, well known in ancient Mexico. It is found, even today, among the Brazilian Indians along the Rio Tapajos, where it is called the baraquita or muyrakyta and is, or used to be made from a green clay, found under water and hardening on exposure to air.

On this hard, green stone idol, carved in high relief, is the figure of a dinosaur and what looks like an elephant with a long curved trunk.

A Dinosaur Mummy Discovered
In "Bad Lands" Of Wyoming

In the Bad Lands of Wyoming, Charles Sternberg found a dinosaur mummy of the Trochodont, or duck-billed dinosaur. He describes this find and shows a picture of it in his book, *The Life of a Fossil Hunter*. The American Museum of New York acquired this queer mummy, which exhibits dried-up flesh and skin texture.

This raises a query: if dinosaurs became extinct 12 million years ago, how could this mummy have lasted that period, under any conditions, without turning to dust? It must be remembered that it was exposed to weather—rain, snow, frost and the heat of summer. The only answer that can be advanced to this riddle is, as has been suggested: While dinosaurs died out, millions of years ago, in the so-called older worlds of Europe and Asia, something favored their survival, in America, to the age of early man, who may have lived at a period in the Tertiary, and not merely in the later Quaternary age, as evolutionists have previously supposed. Indeed, as the years go by in this century, not only may the archeology of North and South America have to be revised in relation to the immense antiquity of civilized men, but also the paleontology and geology in relation to other forms of life. Science has no room for dogmas, which it can well afford to leave to the established religions and superstitions, which batten on the closing of ears and the calcification of brains at the command of "infallible" pontiffs.

Dinosaur Tracks Found Near Painted Desert

It has been said that the dinosaurs throve in an atmosphere of carbonic acid gas, and that the dense flora of the Mesozoic Ages absorbed the carbon and released oxygen, thereby making for conditions suitable to mammals. But if the age of dinosaurs lasted for the immense period for which Professor Lull contends, then some form of dinosaurs may have adjusted themselves to changing conditions, and aquatic and land dinosaurs may have existed in America long after man appeared. It is a curious fact that tracks of dinosaurs have recently been found in stone on the edges of the Painted Desert of Arizona.

Monster-Scared Indians Live In Lake Houses, Forts

It is also curious that traditions of the Indian Six Nations purport that, thousands of years ago, their ancestors were attacked by some type of dinosaur that came out of the waters of Lake Erie, in the night, devoured some of the people, and forced the rest to abandon their villages and retreat to the shelter of their stockaded forts. In another case, in Canada, the Indians say that, anciently, men built dwellings on stakes in lakes, like the lake dwellings in Switzerland, in order to escape monsters who were ravaging the country, though what are implied seem to be mammoths.

The Giants Seize Freya
(by Rackham)

The American Goliah

More American Dinosaurs

In this next chapter taken from Harold T. Wilkins' 1947 booklet, there is more discussion of the idea that man and dinosaur may have once shared the same world. But even more exciting is the story of the members of an expedition to the Yukon Territory who encountered a terrifying meat-eating monster still very much alive and devastating to behold. Their hair-raising trek in the frozen tundra of the north must be read in detail to be appreciated, and the entire text of the story is reprinted here!

Pictographs Of Tyrannosaurus Unearthed In Arizona

In the Supai canon of Arizona, an American expedition, numbering California scientists among its personnel, discovered, in 1924, remarkable pictographs of unknown and extremely ancient origin, which had been cut through the iron scale on red sandstone, and which depict the most dreadful of all the dinosaurs: the terrible tyrannosaurus. This dinosaur is usually said to have been the last of the carnivorous dinosaurs, to have walked on his hind legs, and to have leapt like a kangaroo. Not the sort of beast a fossil-hunter would like to have around while he was pecking fossils, or hacking rocks in a wild gorge! Tyrannosaurus reached all of 35 feet, and is, so far, the largest known of the dinosaurs. Careful examination of the rocks disclosed the genuine antiquity of this petroglyph.

Questioned by the scientists of the expedition, the Indians of the region said the petroglyph was not done by any ancestors of theirs, but by "giant men in the long, long ago." It is certainly no joke or fake of modern origin. It shows the dinosaur erect on his hind legs with his tail extended, as the artist must have seen him, untold ages ago.

Artifact Of Armoured Stegosaurus Type Found East Of Portland, Oregon

I myself possess a photograph of an ancient carved image, found in volcanic tufa, and made by some ancient man of race unknown who once lived near the gorge of the Columbia River in Oregon. This artifact depicts a type of armored dinosaur like the stegosaurus. It is skillfully carved, is undeniably ancient, and not of Red Indian origin. The location of the find was about 15 miles east of Portland, Oregon, on the site of a later old Indian camping ground. The monster shows a formidable array of teeth, has serrated ridge armor along the top of the back, and heavy body armor. The armored legs seem to be missing.

Tall Tales From The Yukon Territory

All this leads us by way of preface to certain queer stories told by trappers in northern British Columbia, gold prospectors and old sourdoughs in the Yukon territory of Canada's Northwest, and Uncle Sam's Alaska.

As long ago as 1887, an American engineer from Washington, D.C., Mr. H. von Beyer, was staying at Port Townsend, Puget Sound, Washington territory, when a mysterious rumor spread around about a monstrous animal seen in the interior of Alaska. The story had probably reached Puget Sound from some trading steamship arrived from Sitka. White folk at Port Townsend told von Beyer that Indians had gone into Alaska and had taken the trail up the Yukon River. At a point a great way up into the interior, the Indians had seen strange tracks on the ground. They followed this spoor for many miles and finally came in sight of strange hairy animals of immense size and unknown species. The Indians were scared at the enormous girth of these animals, whose tracks were described as following a circular route. The story had passed through many mouths and von Beyer doubted it. He suspicioned it had come from some Vancouver Island Indians who had taken a long journey north by sea.

It may be here noted that the Iroquois Indians of New York State and of eastern Canada have old traditions of about a huge animal that traveled in circles in days long before white men discovered Canada. It had been supposed that the traditions referred to the American bison or buffalo.

However, in 1905, another and remarkable story appeared in the scientific journal published in Paris, France. It purported to relate the adventures of one George Dupuy, a French traveler, a banker of San

The American Goliah

Francisco, a French-Canadian mission priest, and an American gold-hunter and fossicker a an Indian village called Armstrong Creek, located near the McQuesten River, in the Yukon territory. This river flows through marshy tundras and alongside hills located between the 138 and 136 meridians, some 100 miles east of Dawson City as the crow flies. Here, in the neighborhood of Partridge Creek, the party encountered a terrible monster that seems to have been an Arctic dinosaur.

One Buttler, an American, and another prospector were one day hunting three large moose at the mouth of Clear Creek when, on a sudden, as they were stalking the moose down wind, they say a huge bull moose raise his head from the moss and lichens where he had been quietly browsing and give three bounds. Another moose uttered a loud bellow—given only when a mortal enemy is near, or when the moose is badly wounded—and the three moose set off at a frantic gallop to the south.

The men cautiously approached the spot, which was partly screened by pines and undergrowth, when they saw in the snow the imprint of the body of some monstrous animal whose belly had left in the slime of a river creek an impression two feet deep, 30 feet long and 12 feet wide! Four gigantic paws, deeply impressed in the muck, had left prints five feet long and two-and-a-half feet wide. There were also prints of sharp claws which measured one foot long, and were deeply embedded in the mud. The men measured the impression of a tail 10 feet long and 16 inches wide at the middle!

They trailed the monster's tracks up a valley until, after abut six miles, they entered a ravine called Partridge Creek. Here, the tracks abruptly and unaccountably ended. It looked as if the monster had given a tremendous bound up the cliff of the ravine. Deciding that the location was unhealthy, the men made tracks for an outpost.

Dupuy, when he was told the story, laughed and joked at Buttler.

Buttler angrily retorted that he and his pal were more sober than most judges when they trailed that monster's tracks. It was arranged that Buttler should guide Dupuy, the French priest, Padre Pierre Lavagneux, a Yukon sourdough, and half a dozen Indians to the spot, and for a whole day the party searched the banks of the McQuesten, the flats of Partridge Creek, and the whole countryside between the little township of Barlow, on the embouchure of the McQuesten River with the Stewart River which flows into the Yukon, and a lofty snow-covered range which numbers Mt. Haldane among its most valiant peaks.

They found nothing unusual and they reported the facts to a sergeant of the Royal Canadian Mounted Police who, though skeptical and humorous, agreed to join them in the hunt for the monster.

One evening, tired out after wading through sloughs and frozen tundras, they pulled up near the summit of a rock gulch and lit a campfire, as evening was coming on. The pine logs blazed brightly and there was the pleasant odor of turpentine and balsam mingling with the more pleasant smell of bacon and porky beans cooking at the fire. The red sun had his orb about level with the top of the divide.

As Dupuy later wrote: "We lay by the fire, relaxed our aching limbs, and let our eyes roam over the marsh, glittering with icicles and hoar frost crystals, that we had just crossed. The tea was steaming ready in the pail when, on a sudden, we were startled by the sound of falling stone tumbling down into the bottom of the ravine, followed by larger boulders. Then came a harsh and appalling roar. We sprang to our feet and I don't mind saying my teeth chattered and it was not with cold, either! Right across the ravine, on the side opposite to that where we were camped, the boulders were rolling heavily into the bottom, as a gigantic black and hairy animal slowly and heavily ascended the grade. From the corner of its mouth a bloodstained frothy slime dripped. Its horrid jaws were munching, munching, munching. The priest, the sourdough, and Buttler unconsciously clasped each other by the arms and tried to shout, but could not utter a sound. And well for us was it that they were stricken dumb! Our Indians crouched on the ground, their faces ashy and their bodies trembling like aspen leaves. They pressed their faces on the ground to shut out the sight. Buttler suddenly got up and tore down the hill.

"Luckily, the monster had not sighted us! He stopped barely 100 paces from us. Then, propping his huge belly on a big flat rock, he stood motionless, gazing into the glaring eye of the red and setting sun! It was a sight that may have been not unfamiliar to our giant forefathers in a remote age. The monster stood still for ten minutes, as did we. He actually swiveled round his huge neck and still did not see us. I calculated he was around 50 feet long. He had a sort of rhinoceros horn on top of his jaws and his carcass was covered with black stiff bristles like those of a wild boar. The hair was plastered with mud and frozen muck. I'd put his weight at all of 50 tons.

"As we watched, a sound like the crunching of bones came from his dripping jaws. Then he reared on his hind legs, emitted a horribly hollow roar, gave a terrific leap, and vanished up the ravine. We made no attempt to follow him."

Dupuy and the party went to Dawson City and asked the governor to send out 50 armed men and mules, though it seems to me that a battery of howitzers would not have been amiss. The *Dawson City Daily Nugget* got hold of the story and likened Dupuy and party to Baron von Munchausen, Ananias, Barnum and Louis de Rougemont all rolled into one. Perhaps the governor of the Northwest Territories suspicioned a hoax, for he never gave the aid asked by Dupuy.

Yet the monster was seen again. About five years later, when Dupuy was back in France, he had a letter from Pere Lavagneux, who wrote:

"Ten of my Indians and myself have again seen that horrible beast of Partridge Creek. It was on Christmas Eve, and the monster was passing like a whirlwind over the frozen surface of the river, breaking off with his hind feet enormous blocks of ice from the frozen surface. His fur was covered with hoar frost and his little eyes—that was why he probably did not see us when we met him, some five years back when you were here, my son—glittered like fire in the dusk. He had in his jaws something which looked to me like a caribou. He moved at the rate of more than 30 miles an hour. The temperature stood at 45 degrees below zero. At the corner of the cut-off, the monster vanished.

"It is evidently the same monster we saw before. Together with the chief Stinehane and his two sons, I followed up the trail of the horrid beast. They were exactly like the tracks you and I and the rest saw when you were here. Then, they were embedded in the muck of the moose lick. Eight times on the snow we measured the prints.

They were the same and so was the enormous body. Not the 20th of an inch difference! We trailed them to Stewart, fully three miles, when the snow fell and obliterated the tracks."

Speculation On The Myth Or Reality Of Modern Monsters

Of course, readers may, like the *Dawson City Daily Nugget*, deem such a story all hooey, if not a hoax. Or they may ask us, "Where are the fathers, mothers, sisters, brothers, sons and daughters of these monsters? They cannot live in vacuo, nor were they unbegotten, uncreated, nor can they live eternally."

To which one may reply, with a shrug of the shoulder, "Quien sabe?"

Scientists and zoologists and paleontologists ridicule these stories, just as they derided Sir Harry Johnston's account of the central African okapi, until presently a specimen was found. Others may dismiss the stories as legends, or subjects for the psychologist rather than the biologist. How did such monsters escape the fate that befell their ancestors millions of years ago, when the oncoming of glaciation and the secular rise in the elevation of great landmasses spelled their doom? In the disappearance of lush vegetation and hot, steamy swamps and plains where the sun shone ever hot and bright from a cobalt sky, and rain fell, as it seems to do in Venus nearer the sun, only in warm showers in the night—how did they survive?

I have already suggested an answer to this question, above, but I may riposte, as a Scotchman would do, with a question in turn.

I may ask: are the monkey puzzle tree (Araucaria), of the temperate zone, and the Welwitchia (tumboa) of the South African deserts, the only survivors of the steaming life of hot swamps and torrid plains of the Mesozoic ages? Did the dinosaur, or the Pleistocene mammoths and mastodons leave no descendants behind them to inhabit lonely enclaves of lost worlds where climate and zoo-geographical and geological conditions favored their survival?

King Kong Lives!

This next section is one of the most thrilling so far! Harold T. Wilkins relates a series of true life, real time stories of encounters with living King Kong-type monsters in the jungles of Central and South America. There is the tale of how an unfortunate hunting guide is ripped to pieces by a large and hairy monster, and another story of an apelike beast who stripped the clothes off of several Mayan women in broad daylight, leaving them stark naked. Still another King Kong-like monstrosity terrorized a village for several nights, resulting in a mass exodus by the terrified natives. All of which combine to give us a fascinating glimpse into a truly out of control universe!

Hairy King Kong Of Yucatan

Far south, in Yucatan, in the jungles and forests of the Mayas, among the limestone ranges with their great caverns, another beastly monster is stated to exist. His habitat is near the headwaters of the Rio Mopan, northwest of Arenal. No Indian will venture into the dense jungles and forests where this monster has his home. The late Dr. Thomas Gann, an archeologist and traveler who took part in more than one expedition organized by the British Museum, sought to encounter this beast. This thrilling story has been told by Frank Blaucaneaux, a naturalist who wrote "Biologica Americana Centrale." I give the story as I had it in Tegucigalpa, in Honduras.

Many years ago, Blaucaneaux and a Negro went up to the headwaters of the Rio Mopan to explore a region of thick and unknown forests where strange beasts and ancient ruins are believed to exist.

The weather was hot and sultry, and about noon Blaucaneaux and the black man pulled up in the middle of a grassy hollow, which appeared to be a windbreak cut by hurricanes in the forest. Towering up in the center of the glade was a lofty cohune palm, of Honduranian species. This tree's large nuts provide oil, and the tall smooth trunk a wood from which fancy articles are made. The hot rays of the sun shimmered on the leaves of the tall cottonwood in whose shade they lay. The heat was so great it made the men gasp.

They were about to fall into a siesta when their eyes were attracted to the cohune palm. Twenty feet or so above the ground, its leaves and branches were shaking as if some large animal were trying to make the tree shed its nuts. Blaucaneaux, glancing at the Negro, saw that his face had become ashy and that he was all a quiver with fright. His eyes were fairly bulging with fear.

"Say, Miguel, go and see what in hell is shakin' that tree," bade Blaucaneaux.

The Negro looked at the boss in an imploring manner, his eyes begging to be let off the job, although normally he was far from timorous.

"Debil debil, foh shuah, mastah," said the Negro, his teeth chattering.

Blaucaneaux laughed and ordered the Negro to get up and go to the foot of the palm. So, taking his rifle in his hand, the black man crept reluctantly toward the shaking tree. He had to force a way through grass as tall and spiky as any found in an African forest jungle.

Suddenly, an agonizing shriek rent the air, followed by dreadful groans. It was the voice of the black man, and he seemed to be in mortal pain. Blaucaneaux jumped up and shouldered his way through the tall grass, noting as he went that some large animal had made a previous track through it.

Under the cohune palm, poor Miguel, the black man, lay on his back, his shirt ripped to shreds, great red lanes running down his naked abdomen, and from his face to his breast, he was one mass of gory pulp. Blaucaneaux saw at a glance that the poor devil was dying. He had been disemboweled, and his entrails were protruding. He pried open the Negro's teeth and poured a little canna between his lips, and the dying man managed to whisper: "Black debil for shuah rip me up. Den run for bush."

The American Goliah

Blaucaneaux buried the black man under the tree, regretting that he had been so insistent on sending him out on such an errand. Then he got up and trailed the monster through the bush. He was easy to follow. Branches, leaves and twigs, torn by the monster from trees he passed, strewed the path like leaves in the vale of Vallambrosa. The tracks passed out of the forest, over a savanna, and entered another zone of thick brush and forest, which ranged to the foot of limestone crags more than five miles away. Here, the monster entered the bed of a donga, or dried bed of a brook, cluttered with big boulders, some of which he had evidently turned over, as if searching for tasty food.

Realizing the risk he was running, Blaucaneaux kept his eyes alert. It was obvious that even an express rifle bullet might not stop so formidable a beast if he discovered a hunter was on his trail.

It was near on dusk when Blaucaneaux stood before the entrance of a big cave in the limestone cerro. Owing to the peculiar geological formation of these limestone ranges in Yucatan, Guatemala and Honduras, such caves ramify and often stretch for miles in a labyrinth of man-high passages and regular catacombs. A man may easily lose himself in them, and to encounter a monster—such as the one who had disemboweled the Negro—in a confined space, would be suicide. The light was dim, and Blaucaneaux entered the cavern after lighting with a match a bit of an old Mexican newspaper he had in his pocket.

He whistled in surprise. The cavern floor was wet and slimy with the water percolating from the roof. In the soft white mud he saw prints, which, he said: "Were like the thumb and two fingers of a large human hand. Each finger was armored with terrible claws."

Wisely, Blaucaneaux decided to call it a day and to quit the cave while the going was good. He had no fancy to come to close quarters with those terrible claws, and be in the grip of a monster who must be a sort of King Kong of the Maya land. On the way back, he became bogged in the forest and had to use a compass to find his way out.

Later, he tried to induce Indians to accompany him on the trail for the cohune palm, and the cave of the hairy monster; but the wise Indians "were not having any." Blaucaneaux's plan, not a promising one, was to smoke the monster out and block up the cave entrance. What, however, the monster would have been doing all the while this crazy plan was being carried out, Blaucaneaux did not stop to think.

It is safe to say hairy King Kong of the Maya forest and caves would neither have kissed nor hugged them, and any glad hand he tendered would surely have had armored claws! In a word, he would have made some of them into what the old English housewife in a western cathedral city where the present writer spent his boyhood, called "prime chitterlings."

Hairy King Kong Disrobes And Shakes Up Mayan Women

Dr. Gann, who visited Arenal at a later date, went up the Rio Mopan, and heard that native women in the bush had been most ungallantly seized from behind by some formidable hairy animal, black as the devil, who came suddenly on them in the daytime. The monster tore off all their clothes till the women were stark naked. Then he clutched them in his hairy arms and shook them good and hard till their teeth rattled. Having completed that part of his beauty treatment, he carried them well into the thick and thorny bush and dropped them in disgust. The women described the monster as of immense size, covered with stiff black hair, and said he obviously had a strong objection to clothes.

An Indian told Gann that his tribe had come on a large tree in the forest with rough bark. About six feet from the ground, the bark was found to be covered with long, black stiff hairs coated with a white powder like lime. Gann was never able to trail down the cave of the hairy monster of the Mopan. Therefore, he waits for some late 20th century Barnum to bring him back alive. That is, if he can find him and isn't killed in the effort! While trying to locate this "hairy devil," Gann also lit on strange tracks in the Mayan jungle which singularly resembled those of the giant iguanodon, hitherto believed to be extinct.

Teddy Roosevelt Makes Voyage Down "River Of Doubt"

Earlier in this story, the reader will recall that I spoke of a "Lost World" in part of the 1.5 million square miles of the unexplored Roosevelt-Goyaz plateau of central Brazil. As far back as 1913, Theodore Roosevelt and his son, accompanied by General Candino Rondon, the Brazilian Indian who has given his name to the vast area of Brazil called Rondonia, explored the western edge of this unknown region, when they went down the "River of Doubt"—later called the Rio Roosevelt. This river falls into the Rio Madeira, a tributary of the mighty Rio Maranon, or Amazon.

The group traveled 900 miles through difficult country, made portages over many catadupas, or rapids, and lost most of their supplies. Fever struck most of the party down, and they had many of their canoes to sink beneath them. Even so, the Roosevelt party touched merely the edge of this blank space on the map of Brazil.

Explorers Disappear During Search For Dead City

The Indians of the forests of the Matto Grosso say that a great cataclysm drove forth into this wilderness, thousands of years ago, a great white race who ruled their ancestors from great walled cities. The region became one of vast swamps and deep jungles where giant saurians, extinct elsewhere in the world in the long ago, wallowed or walked the beaches of great reedy lagoons. Also, monstrous animals moved into the ruins as they became covered with dense bush and jungle.

In 1925, the British Colonel Philip Henry Fawcett, his son, and a young Los Angeles chap, named Raleigh Rimell, vanished into this unknown from the jumping-off place of Cuyaba. They planned to locate one of the dead cities; but I have reason to suppose that two of the party became the victims of head-hunters of the Kaingang tribes, owing, so I heard in Rio de Janeiro, to a violation by a young fellow of a tabu.

Fourteen years earlier, Colonel Fawcett, who was an experienced explorer, scientist and geographer, and far from any fly-by-night adventurer, explored the Caupolican—a region little known today—in eastern Bolivia. He was near the Rio Heath, when, one day, he came on a large reedy and swampy lagoon in the forest, and in the slime of the beach was startled to observe "tracks huge and unrecognizable," as of some monster like a dinosaur. The Indians also assert that other fearsome animals inhabit the unknown tableland lying farther east in central Brazil.

The American Goliah

Ape Man's Reign Of Terror On Rio Araguayan Border

Point was given to these rumors, in March 1937, when a queer story was cabled from Rio de Janeiro. It told of a regular King Kong, a match for the famous monster of the well-known film suggested by the late British novelist, Edgar Wallace. It was said that this immense ape-like creature had swooped down from the tableland and started a reign of terror in the area bordering on the Rio Araguaya. He was heard in the night, on the outskirts of lonely aldeias, roaring like a thousand lions. Terrified villagers barred themselves up.

After a night of panic, the villagers ventured out of their houses at dawn to find dozens of hardy Spanish cattle and yellow steers lying dead on the pampas—their tongues torn out. In the ground near the carcasses of the cattle, they saw manlike imprints of feet about one-and-a-half feet long. Perhaps the monster making such prints would be more than 12 feet tall. What was odd was that the fierce cattle had apparently made no struggle with the monster, which had leapt out on them from the darkness of the night. Yet it must be remembered that these cattle will charge a jaguar or any man who happens to be caught out on the pampas unmounted.

Night after night the monster returned, and the roarings and howlings he uttered were diabolical. A regular exodus began. No one would stay in the villages. Three weeks passed, and then came a report—which I have never been able to confirm—that King Kong had been captured. It was said that a horse he had killed bore on his back the imprint of a monstrous humanlike hand.

Sex Relations Between Giant Apes And Indian Women; Their Hybrid Progeny

In the state of Panama, well out of the Canal Zone, is an ancient stone idol carved by a race unknown, about whom not even the dimmest tradition exists. Close to the image stands the figure of an unknown monster on a pillar whereon hieroglyphs are also carved. It may remind us that in various little known regions of Ecuador, Colombia and Costa Rica there, today, exist giant anthropoid apes, unknown to any zoo park or natural history museum. Such apes are found in the Nicoya peninsula of Costa Rica, but they are not to be identified with the malos hombres, or "gorillas" who have come to this region from places in Nicaragua elsewhere, too hot to hold them. The peninsula runs from north to south, along the Pacific. In the Tarro River area of this region is found a giant, black and hairy ape, of unknown American anthropoid species.

In the old days of the Spanish conquistadors in South America, stories were rife of sexual intercourse between large apes and Indian women. The stories do not seem to seem to have been altogether fantastic. For the old cronista and soldier, Pedro Cieza de Leon says—without supporting evidence—he personally met some of these women and saw their hybrid progeny, whose "language" consisted of horrid moans and howls, in the deep woods.

**Jack the Giant Killer
(by Doyle)**

Anthropoids, Giants and Mammoths

In this chapter taken from Harold T. Wilkins' "monsters booklet," Wilkins continues to press the point that various so-called "prehistoric" monsters, long thought to predate mankind by millions of years, were instead contemporaneous with ancient man, who shared the planet with these bizarre beasts in an uneasy truce that often spilled over into warfare. The hardy ancients left behind many artifacts attesting to their daily struggle with mammoths and mastodons and the ever-present large apes, if only we are open to their ghostly testimony.

Thaddeus O'shea's Non-Amorous Contact With Anthropoid

In 1633, an expedition of Spanish soldiers in the Bahia de los Pinos, in southwestern Darien, province of old Panama, went ashore, and in the woods captured a large giant black ape, of a sort which, in parts of ancient Mexico exist, or used to exist, in images of stone. A fearsome giant ape of this type exists, today, in the unknown and unexplored region up the Rio Sambu, in southwestern Panama. I heard of an American old-timer and prospector who had an adventure, by no means amorous, with one of these giant anthropoids. He told the yarn in a hospital in Panama City, in 1920.

He, Thaddeus O'Shea, had been hunting gold and rare birds and butterflies in regions where the Indians shoot intruders at sight and ask questions afterwards. O'Shea reached a ruined and ancient city, where, in a lagoon, he saw a giant lizard which skated, so he said, upright over waters covered with lilies and alive with brilliantly plumaged wild ducks. But there came a time when he decided it was fitting to make for the someplace on the coast visited by an occasional banana boat from Balboa. Long was it since he had tasted rye, Bourbon or Scotch whiskey. He had a nugget or two in his old poke and a tin of gold dust, and he might call it a day and quit a country where he had found the Indians most unfriendly to men not of their color.

Some weeks later, he reached the headwaters of the Rio Sambu, where he lit on an old dugout canoe. Whittling paddles from branches, he canoed the crazy contraption downstream. Unluckily, the canoe hit a snag in the river and overset with most of his equipment. All he saved were a nugget in his pouch, a pinch of gold dust in an old needle case, and a pistol with a round or two of ammunition.

One hot evening, he reached the top of a divide and halted to make a hut of leaves and boughs. There he decided to camp for the night.

Howler monkeys screamed and roared in the surrounding woods, and their tune was not that which would have met with the approval of the Ancient Mariner, in the leafy month of June. To make things more lively, the cicadas whistling like a small steamboat siren kept him awake, though really he had been long enough in the country to have got used to such nocturnal orchestras. Yet sleep he could not. Still, he was not troubled with the sort of conscience that makes for insomnia. So his senses were alert, when, about midnight, an odd noise caused him to sit up on his couch of leaves. Outside the hut some large animal was lumbering around. He judged its size by the way it was trampling down the bushes. But he had been long enough in the tropics to know the folly of interfering with large animals before they interfered with you. He turned round and fell asleep.

Came dawn and Thaddeus came out of his hut to get water from the river. He had climbed to the top of a bush-crowned ridge overlooking the bank, when he halted in his tracks. On top of the ridge, there stood glaring at him a monstrous black man, all of eight feet high. He stood erect and was covered with long black hair and gibbered at him in rage. Suddenly, the monster raised his arms and was clearly contemplating a charge downhill on top of Thaddeus. Quick as lightning, our hero pulled out his pistol, which fortunately was loaded, and shot the monster through the head. He spun round like a teetotum and fell dead. As soon as Thaddeus recovered from the shock and steadied his shaking limbs, he ran a cord around the monster, which had the chest of a Congo gorilla. But its big toes were human, not like those of the ordinary ape.

It may be noted that figures of large apes appear in old Mayan statues.

Giant Men, Mammoths, Mastadons In Amero-Indian Myths

The mammoth and the mastodon figure largely in Amero-Indian myths and are found in far more ancient glyphs, pictographs, and are carved on idols of far earlier date, in various regions of the U.S.A.

The Oneida Indians had a tradition about a mammoth—as it seems from the story—who invaded the settlements of their ancestors, and, off the shores of Lake Ontario, showed such rage that he pulled down houses and cabins, then forced people to flee from his hell-raising to the shelter of stockaded forts. Warriors were bowled over like nine-pins, caught up to a huge trunk, whirled around and dashed to the ground or stamped into the earth.

This raging juggernaut stayed around until a chief collected men, fought a severe battle, and forced the monster to retire.

On the walls of the Supai Canyon, in Arizona, is a petroglyph, not so ancient as that of the dinosaur to which I have referred above. It depicts a mammoth with a long trunk in the act of attacking a man who, by the relative sizes, must have been a giant. And, reader, giants have existed in both North and South and Central America, where, in recent years, remains, such as bone and patterned pottery, have been found, as in the Sierra Madre in an ancient cemetery in the Yaqui country of Sonora, and far south, along the railroad at Manta, Ecuador. All of which shows that the men and women to whom they belonged were from eight to nine feet high.

The Lenape stone, found on a farm in Pennsylvania, in 1872, shows a fight between savages and a hairy mammoth on the edge of the forest. The monster has his tail erect, in a great rage. He is approaching the forest, and between the trees can be glimpsed wigwams and tents. Again, Indian tribes of Canada's northwestern territory say their ancestors, thousands of years ago, had to take refuge in the middle of lakes, where they built huts on piles because the countryside around was ravaged with vast, hairy animals with trunks.

The Lenape Stone

Writers in the early 19th century were sometimes apt to talk as if the mammoth and mastodon were carnivorous animals, whereas they were herbivorous. Nor ought this too surprise us when we recall that vegetarians of the modern human species are often apt to be more provocative and aggressive than meat-eaters. As experience shows, the fiercest and most gory fights have often arisen at meetings addressed by vegetarians styling themselves pacifists.

The wooly mammoth, as distinct from the mastodon, possessed a long, curving tusk. There is good evidence, both in North and South America, that both the mammoth and the mastodon were contemporary with ancient man. In old Europe, in fact, a well-known artifact in the shape of a chunk of ivory skillfully carved by a Paleolithic artist has a lively representation of a mammoth's head and tusk. The artist saw him in the region of what are now the Pyrenees Mountains, on the border of France and Spain. But, in North America, these monsters existed at a far later date. In Oregon, the mastodon's bones were found near Silver Lake mixed with flint arrows and spearheads. The Ohio Indians said the mastodon went to sleep leaning against the trunk of a tree. He might be ready for whatever enemy came his formidable way. The early Indians in the Mississippi Valley were contemporary with both monsters, and Jefferson speaks of a Mr. Stanley captured by Indians at the mouth of the Tennessee

The American Goliah

River and carried westwards beyond the Missouri, where the Indians told him the monster still lived in the north. They gave him a description of an animal which appeared to be a large elephant.

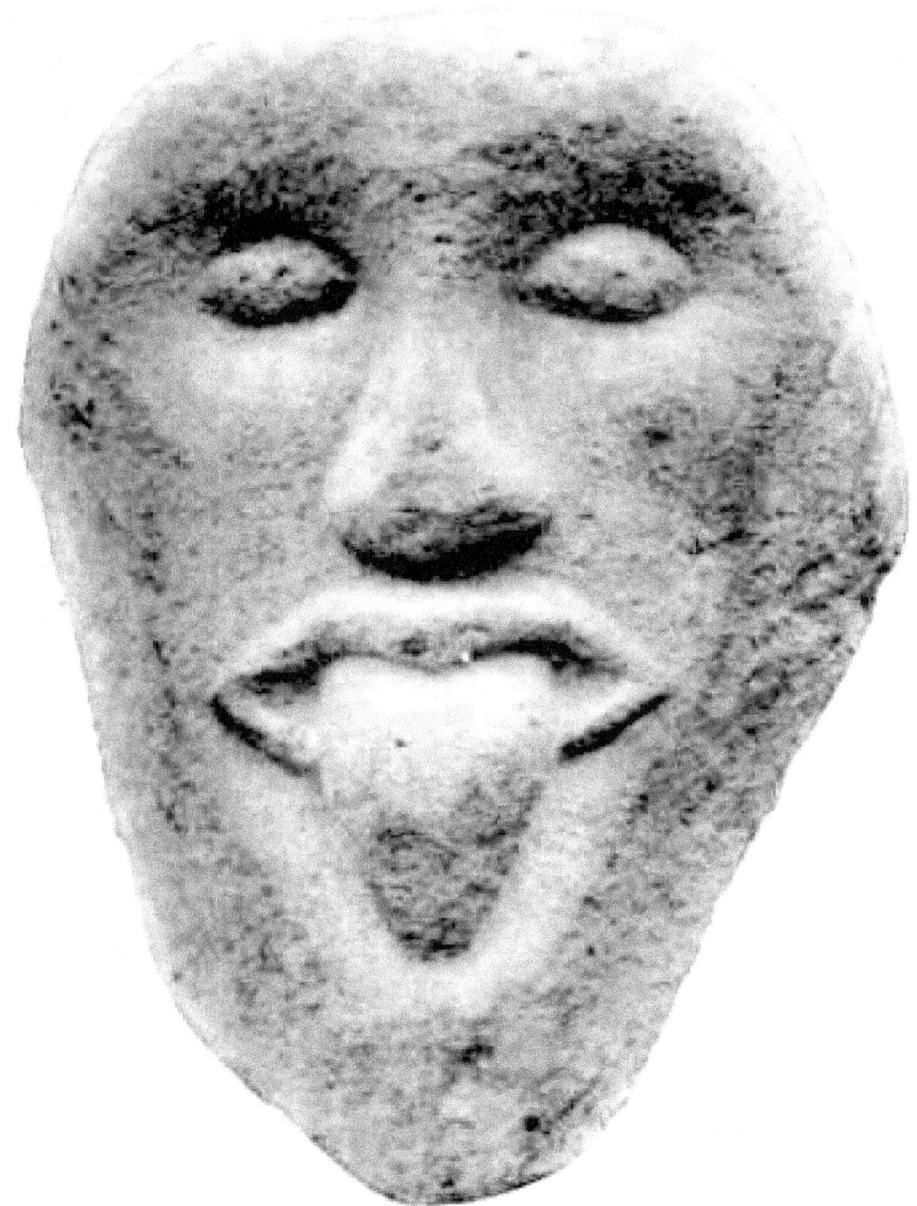

LENAPE STONE MASK FROM PENNSYLVANIA

Do Mastodons Still Live— And Shed Their Teeth In The Andes?

The Jesuit missionary, Pere Charlevoix, in Canada, about 1744, heard an Indian tradition about a monster elephant of such immense size that other species seemed like ants beside him. Said the Indians: "He has legs so high that eight feet of snow do not embarrass him, and his skin is proof against all sorts of weapons. He has also a sort of arm which comes out from his shoulder, and which he uses as we do ours."

Here, they may have crystallized an ancient memory of the wooly mammoth. In remote places, the mastodon seems to have lasted into quite modern times. Indeed, even today, he is rumored to exist high up in little-known recesses of the Andes in Colombia.

In 1820, a British royal navy captain, Charles Stuart Cochrane, told how, when he was in the valley of Ubate, in Columbia, South America, he was told that, close to a snow-covered sierra, towering over the valley, the natives had seen, through a good glass, "numbers of carnivorous elephants feeding on the plains which skirt these frozen regions, their enormous teeth having been occasionally seen, but no one has yet succeeded in killing one of these animals, or, indeed, in getting near them."

Cochrane does not say that he himself saw them, but John Rankine, who wrote, in 1827, "Historical Researches Concerning the Conquest of Peru," said that mastodons were still living in the Andes, and "shed their teeth." Thomas Jefferson wrote: "The traditionary testimony of the Indians is that the mammoth still exists in the northern and western parts of America. He may well exist in those unexplored parts now, as formerly he did, where now we find his bones."

Trappers in the far north and in northern British Columbia believe that mammoths and mastodons are alive at this day in remote regions in Alaska and the Yukon Territory, but offer no evidence.

Trader (Aloysius) Horn Sounds Off

That old trader, Aloysius Horn, whose real life was probably far more hectic and less respectable than the story he put forth at second-hand to the world, was speaking, in the 1930s, of Darkest Africa, when he said to the South American authoress who wrote up his life: "Ave, Africa's a strange place, ma'am. I believe there's beasts still living in the dark places and lakes that no white man's ever seen."

Mastodon Bones At Bottom Of Mine Shaft In Zululand

Indeed, Africa has many tales of these monsters of lost worlds and vast steamy swamps in its equatorial zones. In November, 1929, a party of explorers, wandering in the Tugela Valley of Zululand, strayed up a lonely and almost inaccessible gorge, where they lit on the mouth of an ancient and long disused mineshaft. (Author's note by Harold T. Wilkins: Farther north are the mysterious ruins of Zimbabwe, built by extremely ancient gold miners of some white, civilized race of whom no satisfactory account has ever been given. The race, as to its origins, is one of Africa's darkest mysteries.)

At the bottom of the shaft, the explorers found crude picks and crucibles of ancient gold miners, who were certainly not from among the local native population. Among the debris at the bottom of the ancient shaft were human bones, and alongside lay the vast jaws and ribs of a huge prehistoric mastodon, which crashed to his doom ages ago, and clearly long after the ancient miners had abandoned the workings.

David and Goliath (woodcut)

The American Goliath

David hoists the severed head of Goliath   David severs the head of Goliath (de Cador)

David slays Goliath (Rubens)

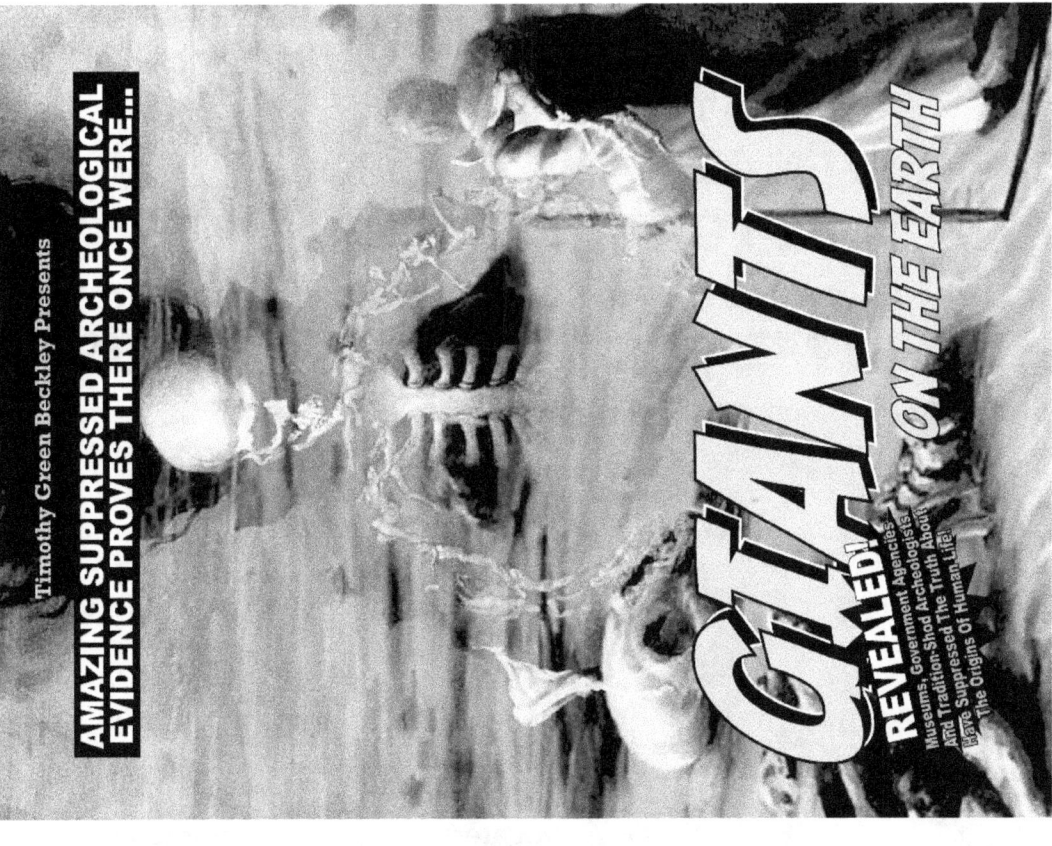

Timothy Green Beckley Presents

AMAZING SUPPRESSED ARCHEOLOGICAL EVIDENCE PROVES THERE ONCE WERE...

GIANTS ON THE EARTH

REVEALED! Museums, Government Agencies And Establishment Archeologists Museum-Shod The Truth About And Tradition Have Suppressed The Origins Of Human Life

THE NEPHILIM GIANTS

Museums, Government Agencies And Establishment Archeologists Have Hidden And Destroyed The Evidence Of Early Civilizations!

A CONSPIRACY OF SILENCE

The Ica Stone

IS THE SMITHSONIAN INSTITUTE AND OTHER ACADEMIC FOUNDATIONS WITHHOLDING THE BIGGEST ARCHAEOLOGICAL NEWS IN HUMAN HISTORY?

· Is there a single, solid, scientific reason they would NOT want you to know that giants—some as tall as 15 feet—once roamed the earth, lived amongst us and mated with our women?

· Why would they want to suppress the FACT that humans not only lived during the age of dinosaurs and pterosaurs, but that giants inhabited the planet right along side both beast and homo sapiens?

· Furthermore, why are we not shown the abundance of EVIDENCE concerning the reality of giants in the form of massive bones, body armor and weapons which have been collected far and wide?

· Did giants take humans as their slaves? Are they still "in hiding" on Earth? Did they grow up right along side of us, invisible to normal sized people? Did they descend from the sky? Climb up from the underworld? And if they are from "somewhere else" will they return, as some students of prophecy predict? Here is a non-theological approach to a mystifying topic that will astound and fascinate the reader. . . YES THERE WERE GIANTS ON THE EARTH!

$29.95 + $6.00 Shipping & Handling

Global Communications, Box 753, New Brunswick, NJ 08903
Credit Card Orders 732 602-3407   MRUFO8@hotmail.com

Contains The Most Controversial Occult Teachings Of The Twentieth Century

Lessons On How You Can Become A MYSTIC UTOPIAN "SUPERMAN"

A Private Course In Universal Magnetism And

THE MENTAL CONTROL OF OTHERS

In 1925 a rare set of books were released by a highly controversial occultist and Utopian movement founder who sought to create a Nazi-like racial "superman" through development of occult powers to control others.

Edmund Shaftesbury (pseudonym of Webster Edgerly) saw his followers as the founding members of a new race free from "impurities," and advocated sometimes bizarre teachings which included a "correct diet" as well as mental and physical exercises which would give them control over the thoughts of others.

The author firmly believed that "One person may be controlled by another without the latter's aid or knowledge. This is known as the Eleventh Principle."

ADDED BONUS SECTION (For Our Readers Only)

We have imposed upon conspiracy journalist Nick Redfern, author of *A Covert Agenda*, to add a highly informative section detailing the controversial life of the author and his little known "political connections."

We have combined the entire text of several volumes into one easy-to-read, reformatted edition of over 650 large sized pages. This rare collector's item is a MUST for those interested in Mind Control, Hypnosis, and Mental Alchemy.

❏ Order *MYSTIC UTOPIAN SUPERMAN* now for just $59.95 + $8.00 S/H

INNER LIGHT · Box 753 · New Brunswick, NJ 08903
PayPal: MrUFO8@hotmail.com

CIA UFO DIARY OF COMMANDER MOORE

"A CHILLING MUST READ FOR ALL CONSPIRACY PRONE UFO ADVOCATES"
TIMOTHY GREEN BECKLEY, EDITOR UFO UNIVERSE

A former Navy Commander and CIA operative's private memoirs involving the retrieval of wreckage from a UFO shot at over the Nation's Capital and how pieces of this craft were stolen from a safe inside a supposedly secure government office building in Washington, D.C.

REVEALED FOR THE FIRST TIME!

· How aliens he defines as *"Skymen"* have been coming to Earth's surface and exploring it for what could number thousands of years!

· Some of these beings possibly have homes in caverns on the moon, Mars, Jupiter, or the asteroids!

· Many more originate much nearer to the Earth's surface, from *"Skyislands"*, or even from within the hollows of our planet, and possibly underwater hangars!

· The *"Skyislands"* are apparently orbiting the Earth in several bands or chains, likely indicated by jet streams!

· *"Skymen"* have kidnapped a multitude of people and skycraft users have long extracted blood from surface animals and humans, and commit mysterious murders!

★ ★

NOW YOU CAN ADD THIS RARE BOOK TO YOUR LIBRARY!

THE SECRET UFO DIARY OF CIA OPERATIVE COMMANDER ALVIN E. MOORE EXPOSES THE EXISTENCE OF THE SKYMEN AND INVISIBLE PLANET X

Read the section in this book about the possibility of invisible worlds — or Sky Islands as Commander Moore called them — then order your copy of the amazing, 275 page, CIA UFO DIARY by Commander Moore for **$16.00 + $5.00 S/H**

Global Communications · Box 753 · New Brunswick, NJ 08903
Credit Cards: 732 602-3407 · Pay Pal: MRUFO8@hotmail.com

THE TESLA-NAZI UFO CONNECTION

SECRET HISTORY REVEALED!

AVAILABLE IN:
❏ VHS or ❏ DVD FORMAT
Check Preference

MAY NOT PLAY OUTSIDE NO. AMERICA

VIDEO #1: HITLER'S SECRET FLYING SAUCERS Aerospace writer and engineer William R. Lyne offers striking testimony that · Adolf Hitler had at least seven body doubles and was able to escape, with other Nazis, from his Berlin "death bunker" to South America in order to begin the Fourth Reich · The true history of flying saucers is a big lie, full of deceit and government disinformation, created to conceal one basic truth: that most UFOs are man-made craft based upon German World War Two antigravity technology as first developed by Nikola Tesla · Werner von Braun, top German rocket scientist, was present in New Mexico as early as 1937, and the "Roswell Crash" may have been a staged hoax to hide the truth about U.S. government's knowledge in alternative methods of propulsion, including free energy. History books and the mass media have lied to us for over 50 years to cover up the true nature of the UFO phenomena.—$21.95

VIDEO #2: NAZI UFOS: HOW THEY FLY Aerospace writer William R. Lyne, who had a Top Secret clearance in Air Force Intelligence, says we not look to space for the origins of flying saucers. Residing in New Mexico for over 30 years, Lyne has seen several formations of flying saucers and has concluded that the UFO crash at Roswell was an elaborate government disinformation hoax meant to convince the American public that these objects are interplanetary in nature when, in fact, they are manufactured right here on earth! Revelations in this shocking video include the facts that German scientists developed a series of circular and boomerang shaped craft based upon the research of electrical genius Nikola Tesla, and flew them during the 1930s and 1940s · That the Germans may even have built a "flying submarine" that was observed and reported throughout Europe, and capable of reaching very high speeds · That, after the war, more than 1,000 Nazi scientists and engineers were allowed into this country to continue working on the antigravity and free energy programs that had begun with the financial aid of the Nazi regime · That the U.S. continues to keep the "flying saucer" phenomena shrouded in mystery for their own unsavory purposes, while they continue to foster the idea that there are "aliens among us." During this 90-minute presentation, the viewer will see the actual parts of what Lyne claims is a U.S. developed UFO based on combined Tesla and Nazi technology.—$21.95

PLEASE SPECIFY ❏ DVD or ❏ VHS

VIDEO #3: MORE TESLA-NAZI UFO SECRETS Vladimir Terziski has gathered a vast collection of anthropological stories about antigravity craft from different cultures. Being fluent in Japanese, Russian, German and English has enabled him to penetrate the global veil of secrecy of the NWO. Now missing from his post as chairman of the American Academy of Dissident Sciences, the well-respected engineer gave this presentation before he quite suddenly and mysteriously vanished. Vlad believes the Germans began seriously exploring the South Pole in huge carrier ships in 1937 and that evidence indicates they built a secret underground base to pursue human genetic and space travel efforts while the world believed their craft were being piloted by friendly ETs. A frightening scenario to the uninformed!—$21.95

I am anxious to have this amazing information. Please send the following:
❏ ALL THREE VIDEOS showing the Tesla-Nazi Connection—$50.00 + $5.00 S/H
❏ Hitler's Secret Flying Saucers—$21.95 + $5.00 S/H ❏ Nazi UFOs: How They Fly—$21.95 + $5.00 S/H
❏ More Tesla-Nazi Secrets—$21.95 + $5.00 S/H
We accept USA bank checks, money orders, VISA, MasterCard, Discover. NO CASH. Credit card orders use our secure 24-hour hotline at 732-602-3407. All foreign customers add USA $10 S/H with payment via international money order. *May not play outside North America.*

GLOBAL COMMUNICATIONS • Box 753• New Brunswick, NJ 08903

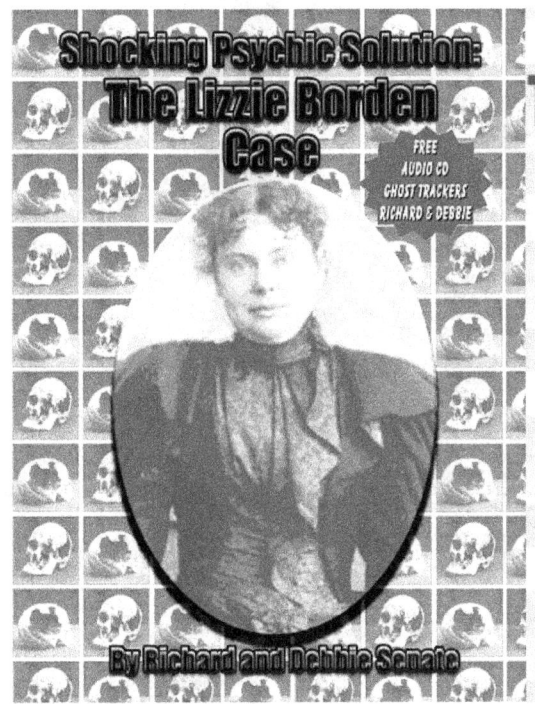

Shocking Psychic Solution; The Lizzie Borden Case

You know the chant...

"Lizzie Borden took an axe
And gave her mother forty whacks
When she saw what she had done
She gave her father forty one."

But, Lizzie was acquitted. So what really happened that hot August day in 1892? Was she unjustly accused? Can the riddle of the Lizzie Borden case ever be solved?

Using psychic means, Richard and Debbie Senate pierce the veil of time and discover the shocking truth. Lizzie didn't kill her stepmother or her father; you'll be surprised at who did.

$27.95 +$6.00 Shipping & Handling

VISIT THE MOST MYSTERIOUS PLACE ON EARTH

**Sacred Site? Entrance to the Inner Earth?
Doorway to Another Dimension?
Hidden UFO Base? Time Warp? Black Hole?**

Come along with paranormal journalist Tim Beckley as he explores a mysterious mountain that has a reputation for being the most supernatural locale in North America, if not the world.

- Here are stories of Lemurians and survivors of other "lost civilizations" who roam the woods freely and occasionally wander into town to trade gold for supplies.
- Little men who seldom come out except at night to collect edibles and then return to their secret cavern homes deep within the mountain.
- Native Americans residing in the backwoods say they have not only heard the screams of Bigfoot, but have seen these hairy creatures close-up!
- Mt. Shasta is said to contain the capital of the subterranean world known as Telos, occupied by the Ascended Masters of Wisdom. This city is rumored to be connected to the Hollow Earth through a worldwide network of secret tunnels.
- Accounts of miraculous healings, including those whose eyesight has been regenerated after being struck by mysterious blue beams of light coming from inside the mountain.

$21.95 +$6.00 Shipping & Handling

Global Communications, Box 753, New Brunswick, NJ 08903
Credit Card Orders 732 602-3407   MRUFO8@hotmail.com

Timothy Green Beckley Presents
Ghostly Pets, Phantom Felines and Haunted Hounds

Elliott O'Donnell
Additional Material By **Diane Tessman** and **Sean Casteel**
Foreword by Timothy Green Beckley

DO OUR FAVORITE PETS, SO NEAR AND DEAR TO US, SURVIVE DEATH? AND ARE COMMON HOUSE PETS MORE LIKELY TO SENSE THE PRESENCE OF A GHOST THAN THEIR HUMAN OWNERS?

DO WILD ANIMALS HAVE A SOUL? IF SO, DO SOME DECEASED ANIMALS HAUNT THE LIVING OUT OF A NEED FOR VENGEANCE?

IS THERE A 'DOGGIE' HEAVEN? AND WILL WE EVER 'MEET UP' WITH OUR MUCH BELOVED PETS ON THE OTHER SIDE?

WHAT ABOUT THE ANIMALS THAT HAVE THE GIFT OF SPEECH? ACCORDING TO THE BIBLE, A TALKING DONKEY CAUSED A WICKED MAN TO REPENT, WHILE IN 1930'S ENGLAND A TALKING MONGOOSE MOVED IN WITH A FARM FAMILY AND BECAME A TERRIFYING MEMBER OF THE HOUSEHOLD.

AND ARE HUMAN 'MAD SCIENTISTS' AND ALIEN ABDUCTORS WORKING SECRETLY TO CREATE HUMAN/ANIMAL HYBRIDS CALLED 'CHIMERA'? WHAT KIND OF MONSTROUS CREATIONS AWAIT US NOW THAT WE'VE LEARNED TO COMBINE DIFFERENT FORMS OF DNA?

COME EXPLORE THE SUPERNATURAL SIDE OF MAN'S BEST – AND WORST – FRIENDS AS RELATED IN THE SPOOKIEST ANIMAL STORIES EVER TOLD!

Here is proof of a psychic – occult – paranormal connection between humans and every manner of species. . . and the ghostly chills they often confront us with. For indeed there are as many animal phantoms as there are human specters, perhaps many more as the TRUE tales in this book will certainly prove in due course.

AND YES, MY DEAR FRIENDS. . .'CATS AND DOGS' DO FALL FROM THE SKY!

$21.95 + $6.00 Shipping & Handling

THE MEDIUMSHIP OF SPIRIT
YOUR PATH TO HEALTH, WEALTH AND IMMORTALITY

Contains Great Secrets to Gain Complete Mastery of the Universe!

William Alexander Oribello With Aurora Thyme

ASCENDED MASTER WILLIAM ALEXANDER ORIBELLO GIVES YOU THE KEYS TO THE HIGHEST INITIATION INTO GOD'S KINGDOM

William Alexander Oribello was the founder of the Mystic Light Society and author of such classic metaphysical works as *Candle Burning With The Psalms*, *Sacred Magic* and *Godspells*. Inner Light Publications has been his only publisher and remains so today. Bill was called to the Divine Plane in 1996, leaving behind a number of unfinished manuscripts.

Now an Ascended Master, Oribello has returned to the Earth Plane to continue his great work, assisted by the mediumship of psychic Aurora Thyme. In this blessed work, Oribello reveals God's greatest desire for all of us to be happy and prosperous and to live our lives as He intended during the Golden Age of Mankind.

These great secrets are available to anyone willing to cast aside the negative aspects of the modern world and accept help from the Ascended Masters whose mission is to bring the Great Wisdom of God the Creator to Planet Earth and usher us back to the Golden Age of Mankind that has eluded us for so long.

$17.95 + $6.00 Shipping & Handling

Global Communications, Box 753, New Brunswick, NJ 08903
Credit Card Orders 732 602-3407   MRUFO8@hotmail.com

www.ingramcontent.com/pod-product-compliance
Lightning Source LLC
Chambersburg PA
CBHW080403170426
43193CB00016B/2790